Alister Ross

Walking Through
Literary Landscapes

I wandered lonely as a cloud
That floats on high o'er vales and hills,
When all at once I saw a crowd,
A host of golden daffodils,
Beside the lake, beneath the trees,
Fluttering and dancing in the breeze.

Walking Through Literary Landscapes

Richard Shurey

with illustrations by Simon Shurey

David & Charles
Newton Abbot   London

Dedicated to my Mother
a lively octogenarian and a lovely lady

Every effort has been made to obtain permission from the copyright
holders of the copyright material used. Should any other rights of
copyright holders have been unwittingly infringed apologies are ten-
dered. I invite such copyright holders kindly to get in touch with me.

Acknowledgements are due to the following: David Higham
Associates Ltd as representatives of the late Dylan Thomas for the
poems 'Fern Hill' and 'Poem in October' and extract from *Letters to
Vernon Watkins*; the Society of Authors as the literary representative
of the Estate of A. E. Housman, and Jonathan Cape Ltd, publishers of
A. E. Housman's *Collected Poems*; A. P. Watt Ltd, the National Trust
and Macmillan London Ltd for 'The Way Through the Woods' and
'The Glory of the Garden' by Rudyard Kipling; Frederick Warne plc,
for extracts and illustrations from *The Tale of Squirrel Nutkin* and *The
Tale of Two Bad Mice* by Beatrix Potter.

British Library in Cataloguing in Publication Data
Shurey, Richard
  Walking through literary landscapes.
  1. Literary landmarks—Great Britain
  I. Title
  941   PR109

  ISBN 0–7153–8486–4

Typeset by ABM Typographics Limited, Hull
and printed in Great Britain
by A. W. Wheaton & Co Ltd, Exeter
for David & Charles (Publishers) Limited
Brunel House   Newton Abbot   Devon

CONTENTS

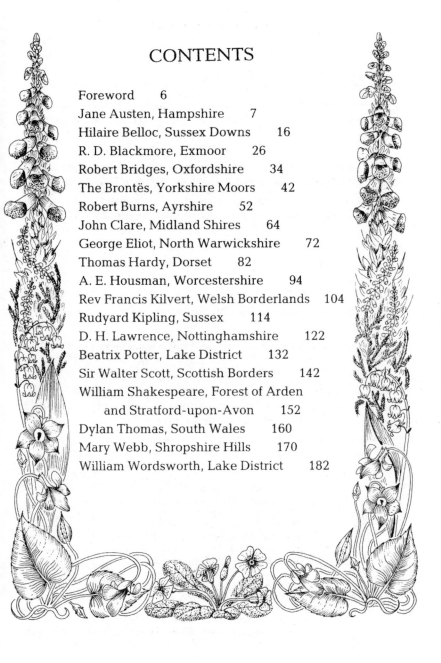

Foreword   6

Jane Austen, Hampshire   7

Hilaire Belloc, Sussex Downs   16

R. D. Blackmore, Exmoor   26

Robert Bridges, Oxfordshire   34

The Brontës, Yorkshire Moors   42

Robert Burns, Ayrshire   52

John Clare, Midland Shires   64

George Eliot, North Warwickshire   72

Thomas Hardy, Dorset   82

A. E. Housman, Worcestershire   94

Rev Francis Kilvert, Welsh Borderlands   104

Rudyard Kipling, Sussex   114

D. H. Lawrence, Nottinghamshire   122

Beatrix Potter, Lake District   132

Sir Walter Scott, Scottish Borders   142

William Shakespeare, Forest of Arden
     and Stratford-upon-Avon   152

Dylan Thomas, South Wales   160

Mary Webb, Shropshire Hills   170

William Wordsworth, Lake District   182

 # FOREWORD

The rich literature of our land is like an elegant multi-hued tapestry; the weavers over the centuries have taken as their inspirational threads the atmosphere, the sights, sounds and colours of the countryside. The immense and unique variety of our landscape is vividly portrayed in the word pictures — from the graceful gentle sweeps of Sussex Downland where Hilaire Belloc roamed to the bleak wild mountains of Scotland, the haunts of Sir Walter Scott.

We read the words of Thomas Hardy and we too are experiencing the turbulent pastoral world of his green Wessex, our green Dorset. The young William Shakespeare knew the woodlands of Arden; here he discovered the delicate beauty of the wild flowers, the intricate world of the animal kingdom and where the deer could be poached with impunity.

In more recent times, authors too have observed their local surroundings — often the scene would be tinged to darker tones by industrial works. Dylan Thomas knew the tough life in the valleys of South Wales; the mining world of D. H. Lawrence was the East Midlands of Nottinghamshire. And who has read the descriptions of the Yorkshire moorland by the Brontës and not felt the desolation, the whipping, damp west wind?

The biographies of these weavers of words tell of their love of the countryside and their wanderings into the quiet ways. To encourage you to trace their footsteps is the aim of this book. If you are spurred to reread works which have for too long remained closed on the bookshelf, so much the better.

Nineteen literary names have been selected — sadly many others have had to be omitted. I have, in my choice, tried to obtain as wide a coverage as possible both of locations over England, Scotland and Wales and of types of scenery. In this exercise I can only apologise for any omission of your favourite.

I would like to thank my darling wife Rosemary who, in addition to assiduously typing the manuscript, tramped many miles with me and kept smiling, and sometimes singing, whether it was sunny or raining! Also, thanks to my son Simon, who carefully and enthusiastically undertook the many fine sketches.

Richard Shurey, Ilmington 1984

 # JANE AUSTEN

The meandering trout waters of the River Test rise in the north-west corner of Hampshire, a few miles from Basingstoke. It is an area of gentle chalk hills, of woodlands and modest estates. It is a lovely, albeit unspectacular, countryside — what exiles in far-off lands would recall as being 'typically English'. It would have looked little different two hundred years ago — the lanes may have been rutted, the hedgerows were neatly woven by the patient hedger rather than a clattering mechanical cutter; the mansions were for the country gentry and not, as today, serving as residential colleges and public institutions. But there was still in those past days the constant green hue, the feeling of being divorced from the harshness and cruel realities of the land.

The world of Jane Austen was comfortable and cosy middle-class, a mix of well-bred clerics, officers, men of letters, squires and inherited wealth. Although the Austens were not rich there was no poverty or roughness in their lives. They lived in a region of minor stately homes, gracious living and good manners.

There were conventions that had to be strictly adhered to, like visiting and calling on newcomers and social graces — conventions which assumed an importance against which politics and harsh events beyond the tranquil world made little impression.

Unlike many of our writers Jane Austen's novels are not based on autobiographical facts. She assumes the part of an observer of the social scenes and mannerisms rather than recounting her own experiences. With many authors, characters were drawn from contemporary acquaintances, but no such parallels have been established with Jane Austen's work.

It is said that she loved to walk — all the children were encouraged to walk rather than use the carriage whenever possible. To Jane, beautiful scenery was 'one of the joys of heaven' — she was particularly fond of Bath and Lyme Regis, but often roamed the pathways around her childhood home at Steventon. She found many hidden tracks where conversations could be secretly overheard, which she could use in her plots. In *Persuasion*, Anne Elliot could hear the words spoken between

Captain Frederick Wentworth and his new love, Louisa.

The Reverend George Austen was rector of the village. He wrote to Mrs Walter, his sister-in-law; 'Last night the time came and without a great deal of warning, everything was soon happily over. We have now another girl, a present plaything for her sister Cassy and a future companion. She is to be Jenny.' This was Jane Austen.

Jane's father was the son of a surgeon at Tonbridge in Kent. He was, on the death of his parents, brought up by a rich uncle and sent to Tonbridge School, then Oxford. He married well, into the Leigh family whose main seat was (and still is) Stoneleigh Abbey in Warwickshire. Cassandra was an attractive woman with a fine sense of humour that she conveyed to her children. George Austen had been given, together with that of the neighbouring parish of Deane, the living of Steventon in 1761. This was presented by a wealthy kinsman, Thomas Knight. So George took his new bride to the Rectory of Steventon in 1764. The following year James was the first of the Austens' eight children. (Another son, Edward, was brought up as his heir by the childless son of the benefactor, Thomas Knight.)

Jane was the seventh child, born on 16 December 1775, at the Rectory. The childhood was pleasant, secure and comfortable. Jane shared a room with her sister (named Cassandra like her mother) whom she greatly loved and admired. The sons were well educated by their father but the parson did not feel competent to teach his two daughters.

In 1783, Cassandra and Jane left the seclusion of their home and were sent to a school in Oxford. It was a complete contrast to their past life and they were not happy. When the girls caught a dangerous fever, Mrs Austen took them home — Jane almost died from the illness. After a year, another school was tried. The Abbey School, Reading, was in the gatehouse of the partly ruined medieval monastery. It was a casual and friendly establishment. A few hours' tuition only was given each day, then the pupils were free to do as they wished. After a year, Jane and Cassandra again went back to their congenial home.

Jane was now encouraged by her parents to appreciate literature. She read avidly over a very wide range of works from the Rectory library. There was none of the later Victorian strictness and Jane even read *Tom Jones* by Fielding. Reading aloud from novels and poetry was a popular pastime, as was playing the piano. There was a great amount of family involvement and to-

The Rectory, Steventon

getherness. Good morals, Christian values and strict manners did not create dullness — the Austens were noted for their good humour and exuberance. There were family theatricals in the barn near the Rectory. Jane assisted her brother James to write the plays and also composed rhyming charades.

There was much social life and contact with the local families in the neighbouring estates. Jane's visits along the lanes to the Chutes of 'The Vyne' and the Digweeds were memorised incisively for use in later novels. The Bigg-Wither children were good friends at Manydown Park, Basingstoke, as were the Lloyd girls, Martha and Mary, who came to Deane when their father was made rector in 1788.

Between the ages of eleven and eighteen Jane had written an assortment of items — skits on books she had read, comedies, little sketches and novels. There was also an irreverent look at the history of England which included illustrations by Cassandra. In 1793, she gathered many of these items into three notebooks and entitled them Volume the First, Volume the Second and Volume the Third.

Meanwhile, the easy pattern of life continued. Jane assisted with the house duties, toured the countryside and, after she had 'come out', undertook the social round of dances at the large houses and Assembly Rooms, dining out and meeting the young men considered eligible for a later possible marriage.

There were many dances at the rectory at Ashe. It was here that Mrs Anne Lefroy, the wife of the Rev Isaac Lefroy, lived. Madam Lefroy was to become an especial friend to Jane who was attracted to her nephew from Ireland, Tom Lefroy, later to be appointed Lord Chief Justice of his homeland.

In 1795 tragedy struck the family when Cassandra's fiancé, Thomas Fowle, died of a fever in the West Indies. The next year, Jane's novel *Elinor and Marianne* (later to become *Sense and Sensibility*) was completed and the next work, *Pride and Prejudice* (at that time entitled *First Impressions*) was started. *Susan* (which we know as *Northanger Abbey*) followed and this, like the other works, was read aloud to the admiring family. Her father especially liked *First Impressions,* so much so that he thought it merited publication. The publisher whom he approached thought otherwise even if Mr Austen bore all

Jane Austen's House, Winchester

the costs. *Susan* was sold for publication and Jane received £10.

In 1801, Mr Austen retired and handed the living at Steventon to his parson son, James. Jane was now twenty-five and the family left the countryside they so loved and moved to Bath.

The six years spent at Bath had many moments of unhappiness for Jane. There were incidents such as the death of a clergyman she fell in love with at Sidmouth; an offer of marriage from Harris Bigg-Wither, the son of a Steventon neighbour, was accepted then immediately rejected; Anne Lefroy died after a fall from her horse in 1804. But there were pleasant moments, especially the seaside holidays. Jane was particularly fond of Lyme Regis, enjoying the social life and dances. She was to use the town (and the Cobb quay) as a location for *Persuasion*.

After the death of Mr Austen in 1805, the family income was greatly decreased. They left the town the following year and settled in Southampton at the instigation of Jane's brother Frank, a naval captain. Family allegiance was strong and Edward, who had come into the fortunes of his adopted father, Thomas Knight, offered Mrs Austen and her daughters the use of a house at Chawton, near Alton. Jane had now returned to the Hampshire countryside she so loved, not far from Steventon.

The same year, 1809, Jane approached the publisher who had purchased *Susan* but the book was still not issued. However, now in a settled home, she again started to write. In 1811, *Elinor and Marianne* was revised and sold as *Sense and Sensibility* to the Military Library. The book appeared in 1811 under the pseudonym *By a Lady*. *Pride and Prejudice* was next in 1813 with a complimentary reception. Jane was already working on her new novel *Mansfield Park* and this came out the following year. With *Emma* — perhaps to obtain a larger advance —- Jane changed her publisher. She was excited when one of the good reviews in 1816 was by Sir Walter Scott.

The creative output was now unflagging with *Persuasion* revised several times as was *Susan,* which was retrieved from the old publisher. Jane's health, however, was starting to fail and she suffered back trouble and fatigue. This would now be treated as Addison's disease — then it was unknown and fatal.

Persuasion was complete and she warily announced that 'it may perhaps appear about a twelvemonth hence'. In May 1817, Jane Austen was taken to Winchester to be under expert medical care. All was to be to no avail — she died in her beloved sister's arms on 18 July.

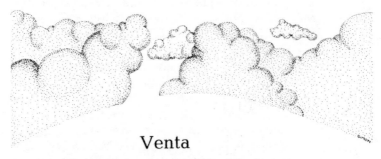

Venta

(Lines composed on 15 July 1817 at Winchester)

When Winchester races first took their beginning
It is said the good people forgot their old Saint
Not applying at all for the leave of St. Swithin
And that William of Wykham's approval was faint.

The races however were fix'd and determin'd
The company met and the weather was charming
The Lords and the Ladies were sattin'd and ermin'd
And nobody saw any future alarming.

But when the old Saint was inform'd of these doings
He made but one spring from his shrine to the roof
Of the Palace which now lies so sadly in ruins
And thus he address'd them all standing aloof.

Oh, subjects rebellious, Oh Venta depraved
When once we are buried you think we are dead
But behold me Immortal — By vice you're enslaved
You have sinn'd and must suffer — Then further he said

These races and revels and dissolute measures
With which you're debasing a neighbouring Plain
Let them stand — you shall meet with your curse in your pleasures
Set off for your course, I'll pursue with my rain.

Ye cannot but know my command in July.
Henceforward I'll triumph in shewing my powers,
Shift your race as you will it will never be dry
The curse upon Venta is July in showers.

JANE AUSTEN

12

A Prayer

Give us grace almighty father, so to pray, as to
deserve to be heard, to address thee with our
hearts, as with our lips. Thou art everywhere
present, from thee no secret can be hid. May the
knowledge of this, teach us to fix our thoughts on
thee, with reverence and devotion that we pray
not in vain . . .

May we now, and on each return of night,
consider how the past day has been spent by us,
what have been our prevailing thoughts, words
and actions during it, and how far we acquit ourselves of evil. Have we thought irreverently of
thee, have we disobeyed thy commandments,
have we neglected any known duty, or willingly
given pain to any human being? Incline us to ask
our hearts these questions oh! God, and save us
from deceiving ourselves by pride or vanity.

Give us a thankful sense of the blessings in
which we live, of the many comforts of our lot; that
we may not deserve to lose them by discontent or
indifference . . .

Be gracious to all our necessities and guard us,
and all we love, from evil this night . . . Hear us almighty God, for his sake who has redeemed us,
and taught us to pray . . . Amen.

JANE AUSTEN

13

Jane Austen Walk

1 From Steventon church and Manor House go along the lane (Church Walk).

2 At a T-juntion (*Rectory and barn site*) turn left to the village and right at the Green.

3 Under a railway tunnel take the footpath up the bank to the right. Keep by the railway.

4 Bear left to keep alongside the wood. At the bridleway turn left to Cheesedown Farm.

5 On the lane turn right to the Deane Gate Inn and the B3400. Cross to Deane.

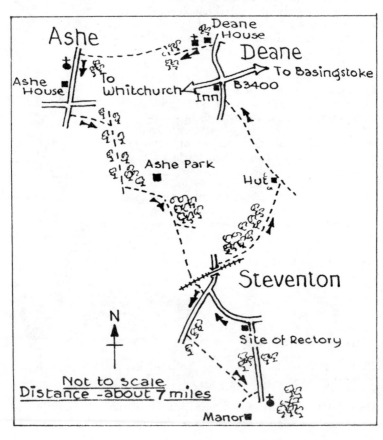

Steventon Church

6 Go left through a white gate after ¼ mile and climb the stile just before the church.

7 Walk alongside the churchyard and fence to a step stile. Continue to the woods.

8 Through the woods turn right and left at the side of a field.

9 Walk at the side of a hedge to go over a ridge to the lane. Turn left to Ashe church.

10 Continue to the B3400 and cross to the lane. After a few yards go over a stile on the left.

11 Cross the field to a bold track and turn right.

12 Turn left out of the trees. Keep by the fence. Ashe Park House is to the left.

13 When the farm drive turns sharp left keep ahead by the side of the fields to the railway.

14 Go over the tracks to Steventon. Turn right for ⅓ mile and take the footpath on the left to the church.

In the *Hills and the Sea* (published in 1906), Hilaire Belloc wrote 'on foot where one is a man like any other man, with the sky above one and the road beneath and the world on every side and time to see all.'

Hilaire Belloc lived for nearly fifty years in the Sussex countryside. Although some of the county, especially its once-lovely coast, has suffered from a plethora of estate building, which has destroyed lovely scenic beauty for all time by ill-planning , much of the landscape is as it was in the days when Belloc lived at King's Land. This house, with its sparkling white windmill, is at Shipley, a dozen or so miles north of Worthing.

The village of La Celle St Cloud in France stands on the wooded heights above the left bank of the Seine in the Ile de France. The villa where Belloc was born was the home of his grandfather (also Hilaire Belloc and a celebrated French painter). After the death of the old man his wife continued to live at the villa with her semi-invalid son, Louis.

It was to the same house that Louis brought his bride, Elizabeth (Bessie) Parkes, after their marriage. She was the daughter of a Birmingham solicitor and prominent Liberal. Hilaire Belloc was born on 27 July 1870. There was a storm blowing at the time and his mother would later call him 'Old Thunder' during his tantrums. They were traumatic days in 1870 when the Prussians were preparing for the invasion of France. Only a week after his birth the German Third Army crossed the frontier and chased the retreating French. When his parents heard the heavy guns moving forward they decided to leave the country; the family caught the last train from Paris before the siege in September 1870.

Safely in London, the Bellocs — mother, father and the children Hilaire and his sister Marie — lived with Mrs Belloc's mother. Bessie and Louis returned to La Celle St Cloud the following year to inspect the war damage to the house. The place had been desecrated and the family, now wealthy after a bequest from Bessie's grandfather, took a lease on a house in Westminster. In the summer of 1872, after a visit to the savage heat of the Auvergne, Louis Belloc died. Bessie was in an aura of melancholy for the next four years. She returned to London,

Belloc's House, Shipley

where she found solace in her Catholic faith.

Hilaire attended Mrs Shiel's School in Westminster and was soon finding a love of poetry and composing verses on many subjects. He spoke French and English with equal ease and his mother encouraged him to appreciate art and learning by taking him to exhibitions and museums. He was also brought up by a rigid Wesleyan, Sarah Mew, who instilled her evangelical influences into the nursery.

Hilaire's next school was Mrs Case's preparatory school in Hampstead, but summers were invariably spent at La Celle St Cloud. It is said that the divided upbringing in England and France and the mixed blood partly explain the apparent contradictions in his character.

An ill-advised investment by Bessie Belloc in 1877 threw the family's finances into disarray. The Bellocs were now in much poorer straits and the lease of the London house was sold. They moved to the rented Slindon Cottage, near Arundel; this was the first of Hilaire Belloc's homes in Sussex. He immediately fell in love with the countryside of downland and beech woods and quickly found his legs as an avid walker.

Mrs Belloc engaged a French tutor for the children for a short time but he was disliked by the family and soon returned to France. The Bellocs too moved again — this time to lodgings in

17

Hampstead. Hilaire returned to his old prep school where he showed great promise.

Mrs Belloc, an ardent Catholic, remembered her Birmingham connections and decided to send Hilaire to the newly opened school of Cardinal Newman, which was attached to the Oratory at Edgbaston. He commenced his studies in Birmingham in September 1880, the costs being borne by a local relative of his mother.

At first the ten-year-old boy was intensely miserable but he soon settled in and excelled at mathematics, English and debates. He read greatly: a varied choice from *Tom Sawyer* to the classics and stories from Homer. In addition he wrote tales and verses. (One of his works was published as *Buzenval* in 1888.) Holidays were still taken in France.

In 1887 Belloc, now seventeen, left the Oratory school with few clear plans for the next move. The decision to be made was the choice of country, France or Britain, in which to make a career.

Against opposition from family and his headmaster, he had a notion to join the French navy. He entered the Collège Stanislas in Paris where preparation could be made for entry to the Naval College.

He was not happy at the Collège Stanislas, especially resenting the lack of freedom, and Belloc ran back to England and his mother.

He was sent back to Sussex to the Manor Farm below the Downs at Bury to be trained as a land agent. Although he loved nature and the Sussex landscape, he did not find an aptitude for farming and longed for the evenings when he could write and explore great books. He soon returned again to his mother, then tried architecture, journalism and politics.

There was a chance London meeting in 1890 with Elodie Hogan from America. She had travelled to Rome with her mother and sister while contemplating entry to the Order of the Sisters of Charity. The moment Belloc met Elodie he determined she would be his wife.

He followed her to America; he ran out of money and gambled his way across the continent to San Francisco, only to meet opposition from Mrs Hogan and rejection by Elodie. Sadly the young man returned to England. As he was still a French citizen and aspired to a military career he joined the artillery and was posted to the border town of Toul.

My Own Country

I shall go without companions;
    And with nothing in my hand;
I shall pass through many places
    That I cannot understand —
Until I come to my own country,
    Which is a pleasant land!

The trees that grow in my own country
    Are the beech tree and the yew;
Many stand together,
    And some stand few.
In the month of May in my own country
    All the woods are new.

When I get to my own country
    I shall lie down and sleep;
I shall watch in the valleys
    The long flocks of sheep.
And then I shall dream, for ever and all,
    A good dream and deep.

HILAIRE BELLOC

With the offer of a place at Oxford, assisted with finance from his sister Marie, Belloc left the army and commenced studies at Balliol College in 1893 to read history. He made many marathon walks and enjoyed physical vigour; he shone in the Union debates (which made contemporaries foresee a political career). He won the Presidency and gained a first-class honours degree. However, he was not particularly popular and was bitterly disappointed when he did not obtain a Fellowship.

Meanwhile, he continued to correspond with Elodie. She became a postulant but left the convent in Maryland after a month. In March 1896, accompanied by his mother, he sailed for America and after a five-year break he met Elodie again. Hilaire Belloc and Elodie Hogan were married at Napa on 16 June 1896.

Belloc's first volume of poems was published while he was in America. He had not been regarded as a poet and the book evoked little attention.

The Bellocs settled in Oxford and Hilaire made some money lecturing and giving private coaching. In November 1896 another work appeared, *The Bad Child's Book of Verse*. It was sold out within four days. *More Beasts for Worse Children* and *The Modern Traveller* followed and were good sellers.

The Bellocs' son, Louis John, was born in September 1897 and in 1899 daughter Eleanor arrived. With the expense of the growing family Belloc looked for pastures new. He thought about a professorship at Glasgow but decided that his Catholic religion would exclude him. Instead he worked long hours on his writings and in 1900 moved to London and saw himself as a historian.

When *Danton* was published it was seen as a work sympathetic to the theory of revolution with Belloc advocating republicanism. His output was prodigious with a range from satirical novel to reviews and guide books.

In 1900 a new project took shape in his mind — to go on a pilgrimage from his old army town of Toul to Rome 'and write down whatever occurs to me to write'. Although the Bellocs were poor he set off in June. 'This path to Rome is a jolly book to write', he said. It was a new kind of book and can be said to have made Belloc's name. The same month that the work was published, Belloc became a British citizen. Two more sons were born to Elodie.

Belloc now wished to try his talents elsewhere and read for

the Bar. He took one look at the examination papers, did not like what he saw and looked instead towards Parliament and the Liberals. He was adopted as candidate for Salford but in 1905 contracted pleuro-pneumonia and there were fears for his life. It was decided that country air would be of benefit. The Bellocs took a lease on Courthill Farm on a hill behind Slindon, near Lewes, where 'great forests of wonderful beeches and firs and beyond the blue line of the Downs' could be seen.

The recovery was complete and Belloc resumed his wanderings on foot, this time to the Pyrenees. However, in the election of January 1906 all his energies were directed towards his campaign. He was duly elected and took a convenient house in London. The Bellocs did not give up the country life and purchased King's Land in Shipley. The village is a quiet place away from main roads; nearby the River Rother rises in green undulating countryside and on a clear day the copse of Chanctonbury Ring can be seen. A mile or so away is Burton Park, home of Mrs Wright-Biddulph, where Belloc wrote much of *The Four Men* and over the fields he visited Knepp Castle.

In spite of Parliamentary duties and lecturing his literary output was still great. During the 1906–9 Parliament he published

Chanctonbury Ring, Sussex Downs

a biography on Marie Antoinette, four books of essays, two travel books, two novels and also a volume of verse.

Belloc was returned to the Commons in the first election of 1910. However, when there was another the same year he did not stand; he returned to writing and lecturing.

In 1912 he finished a book originally called *The County of Sussex* (later *The Four Men*), which described 'myself and three other characters walking through the county'. The work was a watershed; Belloc's roots were now away from France and firmly planted in England.

In February 1914 Belloc was shattered when his beloved Elodie died. To console his remorse, he set off again for Rome. With the outbreak of war in 1914, he tried unsuccessfully for a staff post. For several years he regularly contributed to the journal *Land and Water* in which he commented on the war strategy. He loved to return to the peace of King's Land and took on extra acres, including a large wood. Overlooking his house was the white smock mill, now carefully restored in his honour by the Sussex County Council.

Another shattering blow came in 1918 when Belloc's son Louis was killed on a flying mission over France. After the cessation of hostilities, his Catholicism became even more important in his grief. He had a chapel at King's Land where obituary cards were fixed to the walls.

Belloc continued with a monumental work *The History of England*, but in the political world his views became more and more unpopular. Even the English landscape disillusioned him — 'it has grown to be outside the soul' — and he turned to a love of the sea. He still wrote and journeyed extensively. It was said his literary output was dictated by his need of money for he owed considerable sums to the tax authorities.

With the outbreak of the Second World War, Belloc issued his pamphlet *The Catholic and the War*. Towards the end of 1939 he visited France and the Maginot Line. The collapse of France, so early in the war, broke his heart. Further sadness was soon to come. On 2 April 1941, his son Peter died in Scotland while serving with the marines. Hilaire Belloc did not fully recover from these shocks and subsequent illness, although he was to survive several more years.

In July 1950 a large party was held at King's Land to celebrate his eightieth birthday. Belloc's feebleness became gradually worse and in July 1953 he died following a fall.

Cuckoo!

In woods so long time bare
Cuckoo!
Up and in the wood, I know not where
Two notes fall.
Yet I do not envy him at all
His phantasy.
Cuckoo!
I too,
Somewhere,
I have sung as merrily as he
Who can dare,
Small and careless lover, so to laugh at care,
And who
Can call
Cuckoo!
In woods of winter weary,
In scented woods, of winter weary, call
Cuckoo!
In woods so long time bare.

HILAIRE BELLOC

23

Hilaire Belloc Walk

1 From Shipley church go by the village hall in the centre of the village.

2 Pass a new estate and turn right at a kissing gate.

3 Go through the trees to join a lane. Cross over to the field. By a line of oaks walk to a tarmac drive.

4 Turn right for ¼ mile. Just before Knepp Castle turn right to the lodge.

5 Walk along the drive and over the pool dam.

6 Turn right through a gate to a field.

7 Bear right in the field to a bridge over the river.

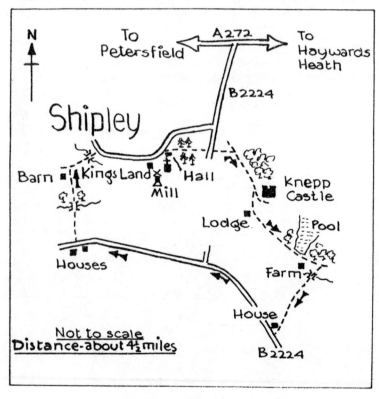

8 Proceed along the side of the field to the B2224. Turn right. Keep ahead at the junction.

9 Ignore the first footpath and bridleway sign. Opposite some cottages turn right through a field gate.

10 Go over the footbridge in the copse. Continue to the barn and go through a metal gate.

11 Just beyond the gate is a junction of tracks. Turn right.

12 Go over the river. Bear right through a gate.

13 Cross the pasture to the left of the house to the lane.

14 Turn right to King's Land (*Hilaire Belloc's house*) and the windmill.

Information
The windmill at King's Land is open from May to October on the first weekend in each month. Refreshments are available.

Shipley Mill

R. D. BLACKMORE

R. D. Blackmore is now known solely for a solitary novel, *Lorna Doone*, which is set on the wild expanses of Exmoor during the seventeenth century. It is difficult to establish why the other novels Blackmore wrote are so neglected — just try asking for the books at your local library or bookshop and it is certain you will draw a blank.

Richard Dodderidge Blackmore was born on 7 June 1825. (The unusual middle name was given in memory of a great-grandfather on his mother's side.) He was the son of John Blackmore, a clergyman, and Anne, who was the daughter of a former vicar of Tewkesbury. The Rev John Blackmore was a tutor at Oxford University. Richard was born at the rectory of Longworth, a Berkshire village in the Thames valley, some ten miles south-west of Oxford.

Sadness was soon to come to the family; when Richard was but three months old his mother died of typhus. His sister was also struck down with the illness leaving just a brother, Henry John. Little is known of Blackmore's early childhood. It is said his first school was King's School at Bruton in Somerset. The early Somerset connection probably resulted from the Reverend John Blackmore's post as curate of Culmstock, near Wellington. After the death of his mother, Richard spent much time at his uncle's house at Charles, an Exmoor village.

In 1837, now aged twelve, he started at Blundell's School, Tiverton; the prevailing fees at the time were about £4 a term. He spent the following six hard and rather unhappy years at the school. He shared lodgings at Cops Court with two brothers, Frederick and John Temple, who did not treat their new charge kindly. It is said that the epilepsy from which Blackmore suffered in later life was the result of the ill-treatment meted out at Blundell's. However, his education does not appear to have suffered; he became head boy and won a scholarship to Exeter College, Oxford. Blackmore started at the college in 1843; he worked hard but still enjoyed the social life, chess and angling. The classical studies ended in 1847 with the award of a second-class honours degree. (Earlier, in 1845, he had been entered for the Bar at the Middle Temple.)

When staying at St Helier, Jersey, he met a girl from Ireland,

Lucy Maguire. She was a Roman Catholic but became an Anglican before she married Blackmore in 1852. In the same year Blackmore was duly called to the Bar and joined chambers at 3 Essex Court. With the recurrence of epilepsy, he switched to teaching and became an assistant master at Wellesley House School in Middlesex.

He developed a fondness for walking in the countryside and also started his creative writing. He tried a novel, *Clara Vaughan*, but did not find a publisher and turned to poetry. In 1854 he managed to sell *Poems by Melanter* to Robert Hardwick of London. The verses were full of descriptions of the delights of the English way of life and countryside.

Following their marriage the Blackmores lived by the Thames, at Gomer House, near Hampton Lock. The house was rebuilt in 1860 after a relative left them a sizeable legacy. The house incorporated a writing room set aside for Blackmore. A large tract of fertile land was developed as orchards to supply fruit to the Covent Garden markets. (The house has now been demolished.)

Following the poetry, Blackmore turned to the classics with a translation of Virgil, which was published privately. He still hankered after writing a successful novel after the style of the

Lorna Doone Farm

27

Exmoor Harvest-Song

The corn, oh the corn, 'tis the ripening of the corn!
  Go unto the door, my lad, and look beneath the moon,
  Thou canst see, beyond the woodrick, how it is yelloon:
'Tis the harvesting of wheat, and the barley must be shorn.

The wheat, oh the wheat, 'tis the ripening of the wheat!
  All the day it has been hanging down its heavy head,
  Bowing over on our bosoms with a beard of red:
'Tis the harvest, and the value makes the labour sweet.

The barley, oh the barley, and the barley is in prime!
  All the day it has been rustling with its bristles brown,
  Waiting with its beard abowing, till it can be mown!
'Tis the harvest, and the barley must abide its time.

The oats, oh the oats, 'tis the ripening of the oats!
  All the day they have been dancing with their flakes of white,
  Waiting for the girding-hook, to be the nags' delight:
'Tis the harvest, let them dangle in their skirted coats.

The corn, oh the corn, and the blessing of the corn!
  Come into the door, my lads, and look beneath the moon.
  We can see, on hill and valley, how it is yelloon,
With a breadth of glory, as when our Lord was born.

R. D. BLACKMORE

popular novelists of the day such as Dickens, the Brontës and Charles Kingsley, who were satisfying the avid literary demands of the Victorians.

He again looked at *Clara Vaughan* (set in London, Devon and Gloucestershire) and managed to find a publisher. It received only moderately good reviews but there was a revised edition in 1872. The work is mainly of interest as being one of the earliest detective novels; Blackmore's sleuth is Inspector Cutting who investigates murder.

Blackmore was not disillusioned by the criticism and placed the scene of his next work, *Cradock Nowell,* in the New Forest. It appeared in serial form in *Macmillan's Magazine* in 1865/6. Like most of Blackmore's books the reception was lukewarm. It has been suggested that he was not an innovator but was content to follow the path set by other contemporary writers.

However, the descriptions of the English landscape were skilful enough to establish a lasting reputation. R. D. Blackmore decided to try just once more. He left the commercial market gardening and journeyed to North Devon and Somerset to absorb the atmosphere for his next effort. Blackmore stayed at the Rising Sun Inn that overlooks the harbour at Lynmouth. He read about the Doones of Exmoor in a magazine — the words brought back memories of legends told to him as a child. With renewed enthusiasm he evolved the story of John Ridd and Lorna Doone. Whether there was really a robber band of Doones terrorising Exmoor we do not know, but Blackmore was swept along by the story and knew that here was to be his great novel.

Not that his publishers, Sampson Low, agreed with him; it is said that the book was only accepted (after rejection by twenty other publishers) because Mr Low was a friend of Blackmore. Only five hundred books (in three volumes) were printed. When the book appeared as one volume in 1872 its success was immediate, perhaps because it was erroneously reported that the tale concerned the Marquis of Lorne, then in the forefront of the social news.

Blackmore made some money from the sales of the book (at six pence each) which assisted his spasmodic income from fruit growing; immediately he thought of another book. This time he placed the action in South Wales, visited on childhood holidays.

Again Blackmore followed a fashion of the Romantic period by featuring a frail child in the story. *The Maid of Sker* was tearjerking and evoked the popular traits of patriotism and heroism but did not receive praise from the critics or the commercial success of *Lorna Doone*. Blackmore now worked on *Alice Lorraine* but was hampered by the delicate state of his wife, and the pressures of the market garden.

Now Blackmore was directly competing for popular acclaim with the young Thomas Hardy (who visited Blackmore in 1875). Hardy was abreast of the modern movements and ideas; Blackmore was estranged from such far-thinking diversions. This was the time that Darwin's *Origin of Species* and the teachings of Karl Marx caused much earnest heart-searching.

Erema with its American setting was a failure; Blackmore persevered to try and create another *Lorna Doone* with *Mary Anerley*, but this too was a failure. The illness of his wife and his own failing health did not dampen his urge to write. *Christowell* was a return to Devon. *Springhaven* was Blackmore's name for Newhaven; this told a tale of the wars against Napolean during the early years of the nineteenth century and was well received.

In 1888 his wife Lucy died, and *Kit and Kitty* was a romantic story where he could remember the happiness of his early times with her. The sentimentality is very cloying in the novel.

Perlyross took Blackmore back to the West Country and was perhaps his best work after *Lorna Doone*. Like Thomas Hardy in later life, Blackmore next turned to a book of verse. The attraction, however, of returning to the Doones of Exmoor, who had brought him such wide fame, was irresistible. Hosts of admirers were flocking to the 'Doone Valley' to try to discover the places where Blackmore set the action of his famous novel. To satisfy this public, *Tales from the Telling House* (called *Slain by the Doones* in America) was written, although only the first tale concerned the characters of the earlier popular work.

Blackmore's arthritis was getting worse and he wrote that 'my walks now are of the lame duck order'. His last book, *Daniel*, was published in 1897. He died on 20 January 1900.

Although R. D. Blackmore is remembered as a 'one-novel' author he has been acknowledged (after Thomas Hardy) as the finest exponent of the pastoral novel of the Victorian era. Perhaps, for this reason alone, it is a little sad that all his other works besides *Lorna Doone* are museum pieces, awaiting discovery by those who like to be transported by words to those quiet and lonely places where 'the land breaks off into a barren stretch, uncouth, dark and desolate.'

From Lorna Doone
Doone Valley

For she stood at the head of a deep green valley, carved
from out the mountains in a perfect oval, with a fence of
sheer rock standing round it, eighty feet or a hundred
high; from whose brink black wooded hills swept up to the
sky-line. By her side a little river glided out from under-
ground with a soft dark babble, unawares of daylight; then
growing brighter, lapsed away, and fell into the valley.
There, as it ran down the meadow, alders stood on either
marge, and grass was blading out upon it, and yellow tufts
of rushes gathered, looking at the hurry. But further down,
on either bank, were covered houses, built of stone, square
and roughly cornered, set as if the brook were meant to be
the street between them. Only one room high they were,
and not placed opposite each other, but in and out as
skittles are; only that the first of all, which proved to be the
Captain's, was a sort of double house, or rather two houses
joined together by a plank-bridge over the river.

R. D. BLACKMORE

R. D. Blackmore Walk

1 From Lorna Doone Farm in Malmsmead village (*parking place*) follow the direction indicated by a footpath sign up a narrow lane.

2 After ¼ mile the lane bends right. Keep straight ahead through a gate and along a signed bridleway.

3 Go past Cloud Farm (*refreshments*) and the path continues above Badgworthy Water. Walk by the memorial to R. D. Blackmore and through a gate.

4 The track bends around the foot of Great Black Hill through some stunted oaks.

5 Cross a brook by stepping-stones at Lank Combe. Continue to Withycombe Ridge Water.

6 Climb through the heather and veer right to Hoccombe Combe. *Is this the valley of the Doones?*

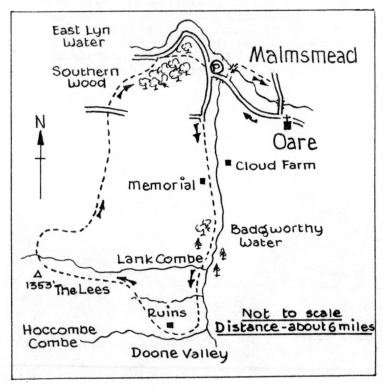

Oare Church

7 Go by the stones (*once cottages*). Cross the empty expanse of The Lees and cross a little stream.

8 Climb to the ridge and go through a gate. Ignore the main track to the right but follow an indistinct pathway over a damp area.

9 Cross the ford. There is now a steep climb to a junction of tracks (signpost). Take the way to Malmsmead.

10 After a mile descend below Malmsmead Hill (*1,274ft*) to a lane. Cross to a metal gate.

11 Take the bridleway to the left of Southern Ball Hill.

12 At a division of the track go left towards a wood. At the road turn right then at once re-enter the woods.

13 Go over the knoll to Malmsmead. There are well-indicated signs to Oare church (*scene of the shooting in* Lorna Doone).

WTLL-C

Robert Seymour Bridges was born at Walmer, Kent, on 23 October 1844. He was the fourth son (and eighth child) of John Bridges and Harriett Elizabeth, who was the daughter of a titled clergyman, the Reverend Sir Robert Affleck, Bt. Robert's father had inherited great wealth from his father — another John Bridges. He was a gentleman-farmer at St Nicholas Court on the Kentish Isle of Thanet; when he died he left most of his assets and property to his only son.

Robert was a happy child and went to an exclusive school at Walmer. He had plenty of playmates in the large family (there were nine children in all). He loved companionship but he also loved to be alone in the gardens, the orchards and in the cornfields. He would also wander high on the lonely downs and along the sea shores.

The poet was able to write later that

> ... it is happy and true
> That memoried joys keep ever their delight
> Like steadfast stars in the blue vault of night.

A neighbour in Walmer was the Duke of Wellington and in later years Bridges delighted in being able to tell that he was one of the first to know of the death of The Iron Duke in 1852 when he was seven years old.

The Bridges family lived a dignified and graceful life at Roselands in Walmer, as befitted their wealth and station, but the contentment was shattered in 1853 by the death of Robert's father at the age of forty-seven.

The following year, Bridges took up the place that had been reserved for him at Eton. He was a good, dedicated student and, in his own words, was 'terribly serious, determined and of artistic bent'. There was much discussion at the time on religious matters, with the teachings of Puseyism gaining in popularity. It was thought that Bridges might have thought of joining a religious order after his education was complete. But his inclination veered away from controversy and towards the arts, especially poetry and music. He became captain of his house at Eton and was a sportsman; strong and muscular, he was especially enthusiastic about football and rowing.

After a little over a year of widowhood, the mother of Robert Bridges married again. Bridges' stepfather was the Rev J. Molesworth and the family themselves moved to Rochdale where the Rev Molesworth was vicar.

Bridges spent about nine years at Eton. He then went to Corpus Christi College, Oxford, to read Greats. Still expecting to take Holy Orders, he worked steadily and was said to be a 'sober-minded' student. Slowly, however, he began to move away from the High Church dogmatism towards realistic aestheticism. For a time the current doctrines of Dr Pusey held sway; he advocated a religious path away from the state and towards the basics of the Church.

Oxford also marked the start of a sentimental friendship with the poet Gerard Manley Hopkins. This was in spite of the fact that Hopkins' direction into the ambit of the Roman Catholic faith was opposite to the path being taken by Bridges.

Sport was still taking up much of his time at university; he was stroke for the college boat but declined a similar post with the Oxford crew.

The Priory

35

Bridges shared a love of verse with an older poet and friend, the Rev Richard Watson Dixon. (He later edited a book of Dixon's poetry.) Bridges also followed a childhood fondness for long walks through the countryside where no doubt many ideas for poetry were discovered.

When the time came to leave Oxford Bridges chose not the religious way of life but decided to become a physician. He was now an agnostic.

Following the award of a second in Greats in December 1867, Bridges went travelling on long tours, visiting Egypt, Syria and Germany. In November 1869, he entered as a student at St Bartholomew's Hospital, London, and lodged at Great Ormond Street. He continued writing and a volume of poems was published in November 1873.

The next year he graduated with an MB (Oxon) degree and secured a position as house physician to Dr Patrick Black at Bart's. When his stepfather died in 1877, Robert Bridges and his mother moved into a house in Bedford Square.

Bridges loved children and he was happy to be made assistant physician at the Hospital for Sick Children, Great Ormond Street, in 1878. But poetry was now taking up more and more of his time and further volumes were published in 1876 (twenty-four sonnets).

In 1881, he suffered a severe attack of pneumonia. In spite of his normal great strength and fitness he recovered only slowly and it was feared that the English winter would result in a recurrence. He therefore journeyed to the continent to the warmth of Italy and Sicily. When he was completely restored to good health, Bridges retired from medicine. He hankered after a country life again; in September 1882, Bridges and his mother left London and settled in the attractive Berkshire village of Yattendon. He devoted his time assiduously to writing; his output at this time included both poems and plays, some translated from Greek or Latin works, or imitations of classical scholars.

The Growth of Love — first published with twenty-four sonnets in 1876 — appeared in a new edition with seventy-nine sonnets in 1889–90. Some of this volume must have been autobiographical for, in the same month that he moved to the country, he met Monica Waterhouse. She was the eldest daughter of an artist, Alfred Waterhouse. However, it has been suggested that not all the romance depicted alluded to Monica and Bridges.

From First Spring Morning
A Child's Poem

Look! Look! the spring is come:
  O feel the gentle air,
That wanders thro' the boughs to burst
  The thick buds everywhere!
  The birds are glad to see
  The high unclouded sun:
Winter is fled away, they sing,
  The gay time is begun.

Adown the meadows green
  Let us go dance and play,
And look for violets in the lane,
  And ramble far away
  To gather primroses,
  That in the woodland grow,
And hunt for oxlips, or if yet
  The blades of bluebells show:

There the old woodman gruff
  Hath half the coppice cut,
And weaves the hurdles all day long
  Beside his willow hut.
  We'll steal on him, and then
  Startle him, all with glee
Singing our song of winter fled
  And summer soon to be.

ROBERT BRIDGES

The couple became engaged and married in 1884 at Yattendon. Perhaps it is significant that Gerard Manley Hopkins was originally asked to be best man but declined.

Bridges' agnosticism did not debar him from a friendship from 1885 with the new vicar of the village, the Rev H. C. Beeching. Bridges, with his musical talent to add to his literary skill, collaborated with the Rev Beeching on a reformation of singing in the Church of England.

In December 1887, a daughter, Elizabeth, arrived in the Bridges household to be followed by a son, Edward, in 1892.

Robert Bridges' affinity with the countryside around Oxford was a constant joy; he loved to walk the pathways, often unaccompanied, mulling over the new horizons for inventive work. In 1895 he completed a critical essay on John Keats; the outcome of many years' analysis and study of Church music, added to a great respect for the faith, was the *Yattendon Hymnal*, published in three parts in the late 'nineties. (It is interesting to note that when the popular *English Hymnal* appeared in 1906 no fewer than thirteen hymns of the one hundred in Bridges' *Yattendon Hymnal* were included.)

In 1907, Bridges found a lovely upland site on which to build a fine mansion. Chilswell House was at Boar's Hill, overlooking the Thames valley, a mile or so south-west of Oxford.

During the same year he was appointed the Poet Laureate by Lord Asquith (1913), and he founded 'The Society for Pure English' at Chilswell. Bridges had invented a phonetic alphabet and designed and cut a special type for an edition of his *Collected Essays*. The Society issued regular tracts from 1919, often containing contributions from the poet.

After only seven years, Chilswell was destroyed in a fire; the Bridges family were determined to rebuild and moved to Oxford temporarily. Robert Bridges was glad to return to the countryside again where he could roam the wooded pathways around the new Chilswell.

Towards the end of his life, during which he had created so much fine literature, the Order of Merit was added to the Poet Laureancy. He died at Chilswell House on 21 April 1930. Today, the house is held by a religious order, but it can be seen through the trees on the walk.

Last Week of February, 1890

Hark to the merry birds, hark how they sing!
   Although 'tis not yet spring
     And keen the air;
Hale Winter, half resigning ere he go,
   Doth to his heiress shew
     His kingdom fair.

In patient russet is his forest spread,
   All bright with bramble red,
     With beechen moss
And holly sheen: the oak silver and stark
   Sunneth his aged bark
     And wrinkled boss.

But neath the ruin of the withered brake
   Primroses now awake
     From nursing shades:
The crumpled carpet of the dry leaves brown
   Avails not to keep down
     The hyacinth blades.

The hazel hath put forth his tassels ruffed;
   The willow's flossy tuft
     Hath slipped him free:
The rose amid her ransacked orange hips
   Braggeth the tender tips
     Of bowers to be.

A black rook stirs the branches here and there,
   Foraging to repair
     His broken home:
And hark, on the ash boughs! Never thrush did sing
   Louder in praise of spring,
     When spring is come.

ROBERT BRIDGES

Robert Bridges Walk

1 From the car park by North Hinksey church cross the A34 to a road called Harcourt Hill. Turn left past the entrance to Raleigh Park.

2 Climb the hill to go by college buildings. At the end of the tarmac way pass through a white gate (footpath sign) and along a wide vehicle track. Keep ahead to stay by a sports field.

3 The vehicle track becomes a sometimes muddy bridleway. At a T-junction of tracks (by an arable field) turn left. Proceed by the farm and join the main drive to the road. Turn right for 1 mile.

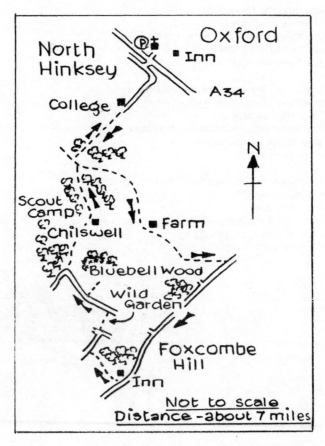

4 Just past The Fox Inn climb a stile on the right. Follow the clear path at the sides of fields and woods to a vehicle drive leading to a lane.

5 Keep ahead to a junction by a thatched cottage. Turn right.

6 Climb to a T-junction. *Here there is a wild garden belonging to the Oxford Preservation Trust with a fine viewpoint up the steps.*

7 Go along the adjoining track to a lane. Turn left.

8 Keep ahead. *There is a nice path by a pillar box to bluebell woods in spring but retrace your steps to the lane.*

9 At a T-junction turn right into a private road but public bridleway.

10 You come to the Border Scout camp site. Keep along the main drive. *Through the trees is Bridges' house which is now a priory.*

11 Stay on the drive which ends just past the entrance to the Scout buildings.

12 Walk along a bold bridleway through birch woods.

13 Out of the trees keep on the main track to cross an open field. Rejoin the outward route to the A34 and North Hinksey.

Gateway to The Priory

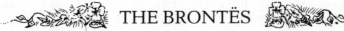 

Perhaps more than any other authors we have considered, the Brontës are closely identified with their surroundings. The bleakness of the Parsonage at Haworth, the wildness of the windswept moors, the closeness of death with the grey lichened gravestones within a few yards of their living rooms create an atmosphere that is so vividly drawn in words in the Brontë novels. One normally likes to walk in fine, sunny weather; on the moors in West Yorkshire it is when the wind and rain are blowing from the west and when the becks are full and the waterfalls cascading that the true affinity with moods of nature captured in the last century can be appreciated.

The Brontës were once the Bruntys. Hugh and Eleanor Brunty brought up ten children in their cottage at Drumballyroney, Co Down, Northern Ireland. It was a lonely place within sight of the Mountains of Mourne. Hugh was a peasant farmer, a Protestant of Scottish extraction. His wife was Catholic from the South but the score of children were brought up as Protestants.

The first of the children was christened Patrick. He was a tall child with red hair and blue eyes. Although his parents were almost illiterate Patrick taught himself to read and write. When he was sixteen, although he was apprenticed as a tradesman, he began to teach in the Presbyterian school. He was befriended by the vicar of Drumgooland, Thomas Tighe; Patrick taught his two sons and later the Rev Tighe sent him at the age of twenty-two to Cambridge University.

The population was excessively class-conscious in the early nineteenth century. Patrick from his humble Irish upbringing to the splendour of Cambridge became wrapped up in this situation. At the time of his University registration Patrick Brunty became Patrick Brontë and one can only conjecture whether this was due to the fact that Lord Nelson had been made Duke of Brontë in 1799. Many years later it was put around that the Brontës were 'part of the Nelson family'. Patrick Brontë was a 'sizar' — the term for a poor student receiving financial assistance. After four years' study he received his degree and was ordained.

After other curacies he came to Yorkshire in 1809 and a year later became vicar of the village of Hartshead. Patrick taught theology at Woodhouse Grove School, near Bradford. A family guest at the school was a cultured, educated girl who was recently orphaned, Miss Maria Branwell. Maria and Patrick fell in love and they married at a double wedding with friends in December 1812.

Patrick Brontë wrote two books of poems at the time of the wedding. There were other publications too — novels, sermons and pamphlets. So from early days the Brontë children saw books in their home with their surname printed on the fronts — the stimulus for writing was present.

The first two children, Maria and Elizabeth, were born while the Rev Patrick Brontë was still the vicar of Hartshead. In 1815 he exchanged the living for that of Thornton. Five years later the Brontës moved to Haworth Parsonage where Patrick was appointed incumbent. The next year, after the birth of six children in seven years, Maria Brontë, née Branwell, died of cancer.

Mrs Brontë's sister, Elizabeth Branwell, agreed to stay at Haworth as housekeeper. From her portrait she looks a formid-

Thornton Vicarage

43

able character and indeed, although the home was well run, she would seem as cold a character as the surroundings of the Parsonage. The town is a grey place — grey streets climbing through grey buildings to a grey church that nudges the lonely peat and heather moors where damp mists swirl. The setting evokes thoughts of a story-telling in the most unromantic folk.

The young Brontës roamed over these moors following the courses of becks to waterfalls and secret places. Charlotte wrote 'Emily loved the moors . . . they were what she lived in and by as much as the wild birds, their tenants, or the heather, their produce . . . She found in the bleak solitude many and dear delights; and not the least and best loved was — liberty.'

The income of the Rev Brontë was but £200 a year; his aspirations of a sound education for his children looked like being thwarted. However, the establishing of the Clergy Daughters' School at Cowan Bridge, on the borders of the Lake District, was a saviour. For the princely sum of £14 per annum the Rev William Carus Wilson, a wealthy and devout landowner, provided a boarding school education for the daughters of clergymen.

Patrick Brontë took Maria (still only eleven) and Elizabeth (aged nine) to the school in 1824 and, in the following year, Charlotte and Emily. Education at Cowan Bridge was hard and uncompromising with harsh discipline, cold rooms and a severe educational syllabus. Maria caught tuberculosis and died within a year. Elizabeth developed the same illness and also did not recover. Now alarmed, Mr Brontë brought Charlotte and Emily home to Haworth. Charlotte later was to use the location of Cowan Bridge and the personality of the Rev Carus Wilson in *Jane Eyre*.

The household of the Brontës now consisted of Mr Brontë and the aunt and the children Charlotte, Emily, Anne and the boy Branwell. Mr Brontë taught his son and Miss Branwell gave lessons to the girls. Apart from their love of the grandeur of the moors the family were creative writers and began to produce involved stories and plays, often written on minute bits of paper which were then bound into book form.

After Mr Brontë became ill in 1830 he seriously thought about broadening the children's education. With no excess resources himself he was grateful when Charlotte's godparents offered to pay for her at a newly opened boarding school, Roe Head at Mirfield, some twenty miles from Haworth.

Although no establishment for an easy life, the surroundings and staff were pleasant. Charlotte was happy and made good and lasting friendships in the eighteen months she was at Mirfield. Of particular interest is her friendship with Ellen Nussey; Ellen received over four hundred letters from Charlotte. The correspondence continued until Charlotte's death and every letter was preserved by Ellen.

On her return to the Parsonage Charlotte passed on some of the education she had received. She also began to write again, often collaborating with her brother Branwell. There was day-dream writing and allegorical tales of fantasy.

It was in 1835, when Charlotte was nineteen and Branwell a year younger, that the older children gave thought to earning their own living. The head of Roe Head offered Charlotte a teaching post with part of her salary accounted for by Emily's education. (Emily was now a pupil at the boarding school.) Emily had cherished her freedom at Haworth; the loss of this at Roe Head made her depressed and ill. She left after six months and was replaced by the younger Anne.

Charlotte was not a happy teacher — perhaps the fact that she was not fond of children did not help. Also with the school fees for her sisters taken from her modest salary there was little left to stimulate an independent character. Her letters to her friend Ellen at this time showed her quandary — daughter of a parson and brought up to strict religious standards, her imaginative mind was set into action to write tales of illicit love.

After an illness Anne left Roe Head. At this time Emily began to earn her own living as a governess at a girls' school, Law Hill, set on a bleak hill near Halifax. It was a very tough and demanding post with excessively long hours but she still found some time to compose poetry.

In 1838 Charlotte, her health and morale at a low ebb, finished this period of her teaching career and returned to Haworth. The following year she refused an offer of marriage from Henry, the parson brother of her friend Ellen Nussey.

Anne took a post for nine months as a governess and Charlotte was similarly employed for an even shorter period, a hated and boring quarter of a year. It was characteristic of all the Brontë sisters that they cherished their freedom — the restrictions of living-in employment constantly impinged on this liberty.

About this time the Rev William Weightman came to

Haworth as curate; he was a pleasant young man with an eye for the ladies. There were flirtations, especially with Anne, but no visible romance. Branwell and William became great friends.

Branwell, like his sisters, showed promise as an artist. Mr Brontë arranged for his son to have a formal art training and, after local instruction, Branwell journeyed to London to attend the school of the Royal Academy at his aunt's expense. After only two weeks he returned to Yorkshire having spent the money provided by his aunt on drinking and wild living. He did not even present his references to the art school. The lad from the Provinces had been completely overwhelmed by the high life of the big city.

Branwell returned to his original writing and to the Herculean task of translating the Odes of Horace. He became an official of the Temperance Society (but this did not stop him visiting the local hostelries). There now began an assortment of jobs and he again turned to art, painting portraits in Bradford. A year or so later he tried life as a tutor, then a railway clerk. From these two later jobs he was dismissed, with drink probably compounding the offending aspects of his work.

Charlotte and Emily contemplated setting up a boarding school at Bridlington and to gain a proficiency in the teaching of languages they persuaded their aunt to finance a trip to study in Brussels. They were mature students — Charlotte was twenty-six, her sister twenty-four. This was a beneficial and pleasant period for the two and at the end of the allotted few months they were offered teaching posts at the school.

However, the cheerful William Weightman died of cholera, then Aunt Branwell fell ill. She passed away within weeks, leaving Mr Brontë and Branwell to cope with the large Parsonage. The decision was made for Charlotte to return to Brussels while Emily remained at Haworth. (Anne was away as a governess to be joined by Branwell as a tutor with the same family.)

Charlotte's sojourn was miserable — she fell in love with M. Huger, the principal of the school. Besides the natural hatred of Mme Huger, the anger of the students exacerbated the unhappy atmosphere. Within a year she resigned and went back to England. She wrote to M. Huger and her fervent feelings for him caused her anguish in later life.

Although Charlotte was still enthusiastic to set up her school, Mr Brontë's failing sight thwarted her plans. Anne returned to

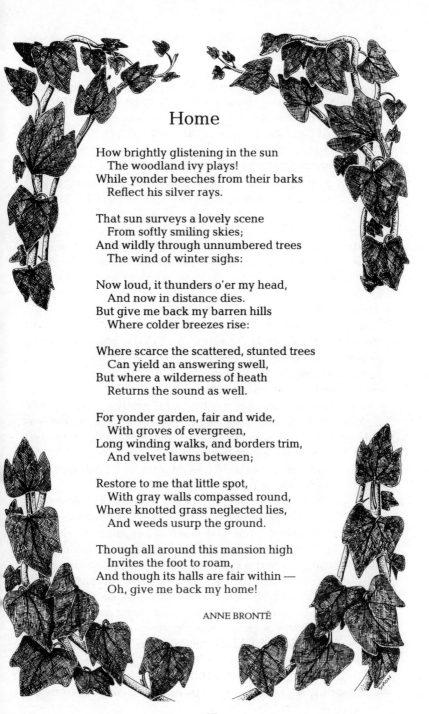

Home

How brightly glistening in the sun
    The woodland ivy plays!
While yonder beeches from their barks
    Reflect his silver rays.

That sun surveys a lovely scene
    From softly smiling skies;
And wildly through unnumbered trees
    The wind of winter sighs:

Now loud, it thunders o'er my head,
    And now in distance dies.
But give me back my barren hills
    Where colder breezes rise:

Where scarce the scattered, stunted trees
    Can yield an answering swell,
But where a wilderness of heath
    Returns the sound as well.

For yonder garden, fair and wide,
    With groves of evergreen,
Long winding walks, and borders trim,
    And velvet lawns between;

Restore to me that little spot,
    With gray walls compassed round,
Where knotted grass neglected lies,
    And weeds usurp the ground.

Though all around this mansion high
    Invites the foot to roam,
And though its halls are fair within —
    Oh, give me back my home!

ANNE BRONTË

the Parsonage and Branwell was dismissed from his employment as tutor; his downfall was almost complete with his turning to drink and drugs. Thus in 1845 the four Brontë children were back together; all were unhappy and had seemingly failed in their lives.

About this time, however, Charlotte came across a little book of Emily's poems. After some misgivings it was decided that a volume should be published with Charlotte and Anne adding some of their verses. The work was issued under *noms de plume,* Currer, Ellis and Acton Bell to counter the current prejudice against women writers. Although a financial flop, the publication did spur the sisters to complete a novel each.

Anne's work, *Agnes Grey,* drew on her miserable times as a governess. *Wuthering Heights* by Emily (her only novel) reflected the lonely grandeur of the moors, the moods of the weather, the rugged character of the Yorkshiremen. Charlotte, too, was to recount experiences in her life; *The Professor* is a love story set in Brussels.

The sisters persevered with publishers to have the works accepted; after eighteen months *Agnes Grey* and *Wuthering Heights* were taken by Newbys, a minor publishing firm. Charlotte's *The Professor* was rejected. The works were not well received and did not sell well.

However, Charlotte was resolute and began her classic *Jane Eyre.* The passion and romance upset some Victorians but was to please the publishers who issued second and third editions within months. Charlotte's fee was £500. The three novels from the mysterious Bells aroused great interest and the three sisters set about their next novels.

The Tenant of Wildfell Hall was hastily finished by Anne and appeared in 1848; Anne was able to portray the drunkard Huntingdon in the story from first-hand experience, as she was witnessing Branwell's degradation by drink at close quarters.

The moroseness of the Haworth Parsonage seemed about to end; but this optimism created by *Jane Eyre* was dashed in September 1848 when Branwell died of consumption. Worse was to come. Emily caught a chill at the funeral and within a few months she, then Anne, developed the same illness as their brother. Emily died in December and Anne, on holiday in Scarborough the following spring, passed away.

Charlotte finished *Shirley* with its Luddite theme in August 1849 and duly received her £500 payment. It was praised by the

Jane Eyre

Flowers peeped out amongst the leaves: snowdrops, crocuses, purple auriculas, and golden-eyed pansies . . . we now took walks, and found still sweeter flowers opening by the wayside, under the hedges.

I discovered, too, that a great pleasure, an enjoyment which the horizon only bounded, lay all outside the high and spike-guarded walls of our garden: this pleasure consisted in prospect of noble summits girdling a great hill-hollow, rich in verdure and shadow; in a bright beck, full of dark stones and sparkling eddies. How different had this scene looked when I viewed it laid out beneath the iron sky of winter, stiffened in frost, shrouded with snow! — when mists as chill as death wandered to the impulse of east winds along those purple peaks, and rolled down 'ing' and holm, till they blended with the frozen fog of the beck! That beck itself was then a 'torrent, turbid and curbless; it tore asunder the wood, and sent a raving sound through the air, often thickened with wild rain or whirling sleet; and for the forest on its banks, that showed only ranks of skeletons.

April advanced to May: a bright serene May it was; days of blue sky, placid sunshine, and soft western or southern gales filled up its duration. And now vegetation matured with vigour; Lowood shook loose its tresses; it became all green, all flowery; its great elm, ash, and oak skeletons were restored to majestic life; woodland plants sprang up profusely in its recesses; unnumbered varieties of moss filled its hollows, and it made a strange ground-sunshine out of the wealth of its wild primrose plants: I have seen their pale gold gleam in over-shadowed spots, like scatterings of the sweetest lustre. All this I enjoyed often and fully, free . . .

CHARLOTTE BRONTË

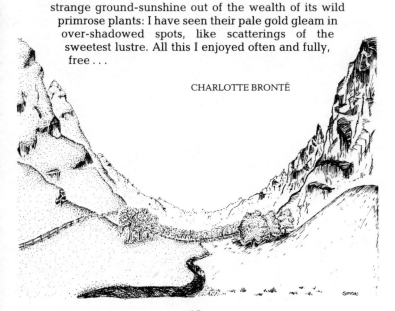

critics and sold well. New editions of *Wuthering Heights* and *Agnes Grey* were published the following year.

The next work was *Villette*. Its intricate love matches pleased the readers but with the use of her time in Brussels Charlotte felt she had virtually exhausted the backgrounds she knew.

The curate at Haworth now was a young Ulsterman, Arthur Bell Nicholls. We can read of his courtship with Charlotte in her letters to her friend Ellen. Mr Brontë was furious at the attentions paid to his daughter and Arthur left the curacy. However, with Charlotte's intense loneliness the friendship blossomed and, in April 1854, Arthur and Charlotte became engaged.

The marriage was at Haworth in 29 June 1854. There were only two guests — Miss Wooler and Ellen Nussey; Mr Brontë did not attend the wedding which was at the early hour of eight. On the return from an Irish honeymoon Arthur was again appointed Mr Brontë's curate.

In November the newlyweds walked to the favourite waterfall high on the moors; the torrents were spectacular, but on the way home heavy rain fell. Charlotte developed a chill and the months of illness ended with her death on 31 March 1855 just three weeks before her thirty-ninth birthday.

Mr Brontë was to survive the last of his six children by a further six years.

The Brontës Walk

1 From the valley *(where steam trains run)* climb the cobbled Main Street in Haworth.

2 Go near the Black Bull Inn *(Branwell's inn)* to the church, Parsonage and museum.

3 Take the path signed Haworth Moor.

4 Through a metal gate proceed to a crossroads of tracks.

5 Turn right to the farm. Walk by the wall to a lane.

6 Cross the lane. Bear slightly left towards ridged uplands.

7 Cross the other tracks to pass near trig point (Penistone Hill).

8 Walk towards the boulders and turn right by a post. The quarry is now on the left. At the road turn right.

9 Proceed left at the sign Brontë Waterfalls.

10 At the falls turn left — they are now on the left. Walk by a stream past the head of the falls.

11 Go over the bridges to a vehicle track by the shooting butts. Turn left to the lane.

12 Turn right then left (Upper Marsh Lane). Go right along the path near Lily Hall Farm.

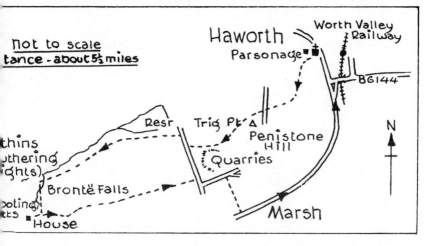

51

Haworth Parsonage

13 Climb a stone stile to a meadow then pass through a squeeze stile to the lane at Marsh.

14 Turn left along the road to Haworth.

Information
Brontë Museum is open daily from April to October.

 # ROBERT BURNS

In the preface to the *Edinburgh Edition* of his poems, Robert Burns addressed himself as a believer in honest rusticity. 'I was bred to the plough and am independent', he avers. His views of the countryside he knew and loved in Ayrshire were those of the practical, working farmer rather than those of a poet of the Romantic Age of literature.

Burns wrote essentially not of the hills, valleys and mountains, but of the basic places where man passionately and diligently tills the soil and with equal fervour loves the country lasses. Equally popular with the poet was his recollection of the places of historic Scottish interest.

In the years after the death of Burns, poets and writers followed in the sentimental vein — their works were saturated with nostalgia for the traditional, sentimental and idealised picture of rural life in Scotland. Critics have sometimes blamed Burns for his rather mawkish facet of the nation that is still in evidence today. This accusation is unfair — Burns wrote with honesty of the life he knew and expressed the view of the avowed 'independent'.

Robert Burns was born on 25 January 1759 in a thatch-roofed cottage that fronts the road at Alloway. Alloway is now a suburb of Ayr but at the end of the eighteenth century it was a village in an area of poor agricultural land.

A contemporary record tells the countryside 'appeared dark and rough, consisting greatly of heath, moss, patches of straggling wood and rudely cultivated grounds'. Another states that with 'the climate rainy, the land clay and having early frosts in the autumn, the practice of corn husbandry is attended with many difficulties'.

The cottage at Alloway was built of clay by Robert's father, William. It is said that part of it fell down when Robert was barely a week old. William Burnes (how he spelt his name) was head gardener on the estate of a wealthy retired doctor. He married Agnes Brown, the daughter of a tenant farmer. She was said to have been full of energy and lived to be almost ninety.

In 1765, when Robert was six, his father took over the lease of the seventy-acre Mount Oliphant Farm. It was hungry and ill-drained land and productive agriculture was difficult.

William Burnes was an enthusiastic reader and a God-fearing man. He was keen to convey these traits to his children; his wife was almost illiterate but made a good farmer's wife. She sang the old traditional airs at her work; in later years Burns was to rediscover the almost-forgotten melodies and verses with such enthusiasm, an interest that was perhaps kindled at his mother's knee.

The formal education of Robert Burns started when he was still at Alloway, at Alloway Main School, a mile's distance from his home. He was taught, together with his younger brother Gilbert, by John Murdoch, who was hired by William Burnes and his neighbours. Robert and Gilbert were considered excellent at reading and 'tolerable' at writing in the standard English. There was no teaching of the literature of Scotland. After about two years, Murdoch gave up teaching his young charges at Alloway. Robert was given tuition in handwriting for a short time at a school at Dalrymple, but, in 1773, following Murdoch's appointment at an establishment at Ayr, Robert Burns was sent to him as a boarder.

Burns' Cottage, Alloway

Auld Brig o' Doon, Alloway

Burns was further instructed in English grammar and started to learn French. Soon his father needed help on the farm and he was called home. This was not the end of his education as William Burnes encouraged him to read novels and historical books.

By the time Robert was fourteen and working hard on the land, there were seven children in the Burnes household. Food was not plentiful and it was realised that the purchase of the farm resulted from unscrupulous information given by the seller. It was thought that the exhausting work and poor food may have caused the rheumatic trouble that was to afflict Robert throughout his life.

When he was around fifteen (and toiling, in his own words, as a galley slave') he started writing poetry. About the same time, William Burnes, still wishing to further his son's knowledge, took Robert 'to a noted school to learn mensuration, surveying, and dialling.' This was at Kirkoswald on the coast south-west of Ayr. He learnt much about life at this place, frequenting the taverns and meeting the girls. Returning home, his amorous exploits continued and he was moved to compose verses of love. 'I never had the least thought or inclination of turning poet 'til I got once heartily in love and then rhyme and song were in a manner the spontaneous language of my heart.'

In 1777, when Robert was eighteen, the family moved to the larger Lochlie Farm, Ayrshire. Contemporary prints confirm the run-down appearance of the place but the family were comparatively happy here in spite of the unrewarding hard labour on the land. Robert stimulated his intellect by reading and attending debating societies and found solace by falling in and out of love. 'Vive l'amour et vive la bagatelle were my sole principles of action', he wrote.

In 1780 he met a servant at a neighbouring house, Alison Begbie; she was the daughter of a farmer. Burns took her love letters as an invitation for him to propose but this suggestion of marriage was rejected.

He became a mason in 1781 and in the summer of that year went to Irvine to gain knowledge of the new linen industry. At Lochlie Farm the family had experimented in flax-growing. Irvine was a large seaport and Burns met worldly wise sailors and smugglers. He was particularly friendly with Richard Brown. Brown was an educated naval man who had a winning way with women that was admired by Burns. Brown, in turn, praised Burns' poetry and spurred him to write seriously when he had all but given up composing verses.

After the decline in the Lochlie Farm's fortunes, William Burnes was declared bankrupt and died in February 1784. The brothers, Robert and Gilbert, rented a farm at Mossgiel, between Mauchline and Lochlie. Although they had studied the ways of husbandry, the soil was again poor and the land unprofitable, and money was lost. Robert was careful and frugal with his spending but liberal with his love.

The first of his many children born out of wedlock was the result of a relationship with a servant girl at the farm in 1785; the daughter was brought up by Robert's mother. The experiences of his amorous adventures gave him the stimulus to compose many sensitive passionate poems and songs. However, in his days of depression, he wrote serious and sometimes melancholic work and included them in his *Commonplace Book.*

In 1786 another girl became pregnant. Jean Armour was the attractive daughter of a master mason and, after she bore twins, Burns 'married' her by the Scots law of 'declaration of intent'. Following great opposition from Jean's parents the couple's

My Luve

O my Luve is like a red, red rose,
   That's newly sprung in June:
O my Luve is like the melodie,
   That's sweetly played in tune.

As fair art thou, my bonie lass,
   So deep in luve am I;
And I will luve thee still, my dear,
   Till a' the seas gang dry.

Till a' the seas gang dry, my dear,
   And the rocks melt wi' the sun;
And I will luve thee still, my dear,
   While the sands o' life shall run.

And fare-thee-weel, my only Luve!
   And fare-thee-weel a while!
And I will come again, my Luve,
   Tho' it were ten thousand mile.

ROBERT BURNS

marriage was laid aside in the eyes of the Church. Robert was again a bachelor, albeit a sad one, still with a great feeling for his Jean.

The pressure from the Armour family made Robert Burns think of emigrating. In anticipation of his departure he arranged for a printer in Kilmarnock to prepare a book of *Scotch Poems*. Perhaps the great success of the work changed his mind about leaving the country — perhaps it was the idea to join the Excise service. The poems, in a combination of the colloquial Old Scots language and the contemporary English style, were enthusiastically received by rich and poor; Burns was now the great national poet. Edinburgh received him with adulation and Burns arranged the publication of a second edition.

He was wanted everywhere, this remarkable man, this ploughman poet. He was wined and dined, furthered his masonic associations but was not averse to repeating bawdy songs and anecdotes.

Burns was introduced to William Creech, who was to become his literary agent and publish a new selection of poems, the *Edinburgh Edition*. However, it is estimated that the total he ever received for his poetic books was about £1,000. There were several songs in the new work — an idiom that was to play an important part in Burns' later life.

He continued to praise the charms of the ladies he met; several bore his children but the romance with Mrs Agnes M'Lehose from 1787 was significant. She was deeply religious and could please the poet by sharp repartee rather than by physical stimulation.

Burns was offered the lease of a farm at Ellisland near Dumfries by an admiring and wealthy banker but deferred a decision after remembering the hard, unrewarding agricultural work of the past. Instead, he preferred to travel and toured the Highlands and historical sites.

Always he listened for the old ballads — the ditties of love and work; he was about to begin his serious study and collection of the traditional Scottish folk songs. He was asked to assist a fellow enthusiastic collector, James Johnson, in publishing a work that was to be entitled *The Scots Musical Museum*. It was followed by *Select Scottish Airs*.

Now Burns' talents were primarily directed to the furtherance of songs of travel and the countryside, work and love. His

Burns' Museum, Dumfries

output of poetry diminished (although the celebrated narrative poem, 'Tam O'Shanter', appeared in 1791).

So it is today Burns is probably wider known for ballads than for his verse. We are moved by such lovely songs — 'O whistle and I'll come to ye, my lad', 'O my Luve's like a red, red, rose', 'John Anderson, My Jo', 'Ye banks and braes o' bonny Doon'. There is also that universal song of friendship 'Auld Lang Syne' and my especial favourite, 'Ae fond kiss, and then we sever', written for the impending departure of Mrs M'Lehose, returning to her husband.

In 1788, Burns again acknowledged Jean Armour as his wife and took up the banker's offer of the Ellisland farm on the banks of the River Nith. He still hankered after an Excise job and, duly commissioned the following year, combined the duties with his farming. The farm land was poor and in the most miserable state of exhaustion' and it was his good fortune that income was forthcoming from the enjoyable revenue work.

Within three years he had given up the lease of the farm and the Burns family (including his many children) found a house at Mill Street, Dumfries. (The street was later renamed Burns Street and the old house is now a museum.) It was here that he died of rheumatic fever on 21 July 1796; he was buried in the churchyard of St Michael's Church, Dumfries.

59

To a Mouse
On turning her up in her nest with the plough

Wee, sleekit, cowrin, tim'rous beastie,
O, what a panic's in thy breastie!
Thou need na start awa sae hasty,
    Wi' bickering brattle!
I wad be laith to rin an' chase thee,
    Wi' murd'ring pattle![1]

I'm truly sorry man's dominion,
Has broken nature's social union,
An' justifies that ill opinion,
    Which makes thee startle
At me, thy poor, earth-born companion,
    An' fellow-mortal!

I doubt na, whiles, but thou may thieve;
What then? poor beastie thou maun live!
A daimen icker in a thrave[2]
    'S a sma' request;
I'll get a blessin wi' the lave,[3]
    An' never miss't!

Thy wee bit housie, too, in ruin!
It's silly wa's the winds are strewin!
An' naething, now, to big a new ane,
    O' foggage[4] green!
An' bleak December's winds ensuin,
    Baith snell[5] an' keen!

Thou saw the fields laid bare an' waste,
An' weary winter comin' fast,
An' cozie here, beneath the blast,
    Thou thought to dwell —
Till crash! the cruel coulter past
    Out thro' thy cell.

That wee bit heap o' leaves an' stibble,
Has cost thee mony a weary nibble!
Now thou's turn'd out, for a' thy trouble,
But house or hald,[6]
To thole the winter's sleety dribble,
An' cranreuch[7] cauld!

But, Mousie, thou art no thy lane,[8]
In proving foresight may be vain;
The best-laid schemes o' mice an men
Gang aft a-gley,
An' lea'e us naught but grief an' pain,
For promised joy!

Still thou art blest, compared wi' me;
The present only toucheth thee:
But och! I backward cast me e'e,
On prospects drear!
An'forward, tho' I canna see,
I guess an' fear!

ROBERT BURNS

1 Plough-stick
2 An odd ear of wheat in a shock of grain
3 The leavings
4 Moss
5 Sharp
6 Without house or home
7 Hoar-frost
8 Not the only one

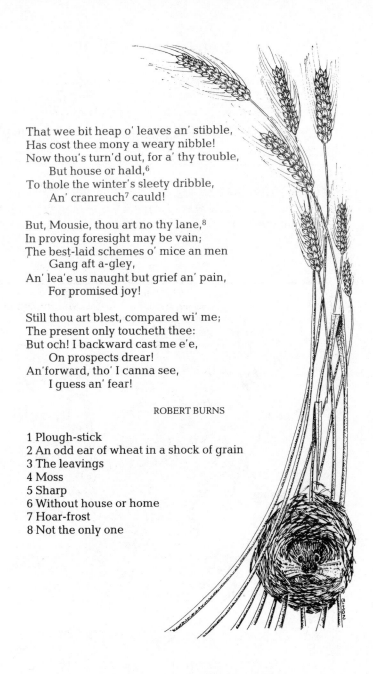

Robert Burns Walk

1 From the car park by Burns' Cottage walk along the B7024 to Burns Centre, Old Kirk *(Burns' father's grave)* and Auld Brig O' Doon. *Nearby is Burns' monument.*

2 Retrace your steps along the B7024. Turn left at Shanter Way and keep ahead to the woods. At once turn left down the steps to the river.

3 Turn right. Stay by the river downstream until the track climbs to a vehicle way. Turn left to the road then left again to join the A719.

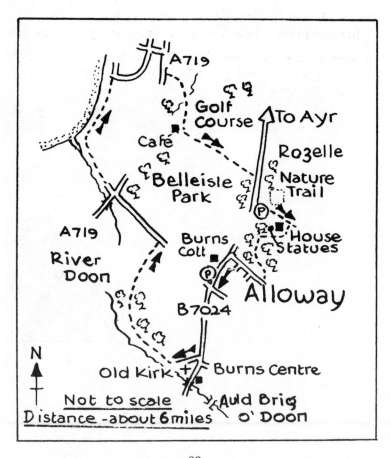

4 Cross directly over to a hard vehicle track to the seashore. *The spectacularly sited building on the clifftop to the left is Greenan Castle.*

5 Turn right along the beach to the road. Turn right (Auchendon Crescent), and right again to the A719.

6 Turn right to the lodge gate of Belleisle Park. Follow the tarmac way to the club house.

7 At the signpost (Rozelle) cross the golf course to the B7024. Turn right. Enter the park *(nature trail; house, built 1750 and art gallery).*

8 Past the front of the house turn right through a gateway (no gate) to the lawns.

9 Walk by unusual statues by Ronald Rae. Go through a railing gate to the woods. Turn left at the crossing of the tracks.

10 Keep on the path just inside the wood (grass on the left side). By a small latch gate after ½ mile turn right through a gap in a wire fence.

11 Turn right. Follow the path at the edge of the woods to Burness Avenue. Turn right to the B7024. The car park is on the left.

Information
Burns' Cottage is open daily from 10.00am to 5.00pm.

By his own admission, Helpston in Northamptonshire, where John Clare was born a twin on 13 July 1793, was 'a gloomy village on the brink of the Lincolnshire Fens'.

The region is flat and enclosure of the open fields had not yet started. The idea of enclosure was to make agriculture more economic than the ridge and furrow strip farming and to improve the soil, but there is no evidence to suggest the Clares were paupers.

John Clare was the son of a flail-thresher, Parker Clare, who also earned some money as a singer of folk songs and as a wrestler. When Parker was born his Scottish father, being un-married, fled from the area.

John's mother was Ann Stimson, daughter of a shepherd from nearby Castor. Like her husband she, too, sang the old songs that had been handed down from her forefathers. Sing-ing at work was a tradition that ensured the preservation of folk song. Clare said his father knew 'over a hundred ballads', which he sang at the festivals and May fairs.

John's twin sister died within weeks of being born; John was said to have been a weakling and it was a surprise that he was the one to survive. Another child also died in infancy, leaving two children — a small family indeed in those days.

His mother was keen to see her children educated. When a child, John assisted in the threshing of the grain, using a small flail tailor-made for him by his father. With the money earned John paid for some schooling — he attended a dame school in Helpston for three months each year from the age of five to seven. His next school was held in the church vestry at Glinton, two lonely miles away. John was an avid reader at home and, with a prodigious gift, could memorise long sections of books.

During the time at Glinton he fell in love with young Mary Joyce, who came from a comfortably-off family. In his *Notes for my Life* he tells of his affections and of his walks into the coun-tryside with her; they roamed through the meadows and by the brook.

While still only twelve, John Clare was enthusiastically com-posing poetry, influenced by his parents singing verses in their folk songs. 'I cannot say . . . at what age I began to write it

John Clare's Birthplace

[poetry] . . . but my first feelings and attempts . . . were imitations of my father's songs . . .'

He was loaned Thomson's *The Seasons* and this was a great influence on his rustic thoughts. He was determined to get a copy himself (at one shilling and sixpence). He obtained the money from his father and walked into Stamford to the booksellers. With his copy of *The Seasons* John started his collection of poetry books that he was to treasure for life. Meanwhile, he wrote with enthusiasm himself.

Just after he left school his father was struck down with rheumatism — a common disease on the damp of the Fenlands. John was now to assist with the family finances. Next to the Clares' cottage was the Blue Bell Inn and John secured the job of house-boy to the landlord.

After a year he became a plough-boy at Woodcroft Castle for the Bellair family. He witnessed an accident; a worker falling to his death from a wagon was said to have caused the start of John's fainting fits. Again he only stayed in the post a year and wished to better himself. He considered being apprenticed to a cobbler or working in a lawyer's office, but settled for a gardening situation at Burghley House, a place that necessitated his living away from home. Clare was becoming a lonely character, enjoying the solitude with nature. He left Burghley House and journeyed to Newark.

65

St Botholph's, Helpston

At this time (1812), the invasion by Napoleon seemed imminent and volunteers were being sought to join the defensive
army. The nineteen-year-old Clare received his two-guinea
bounty and signed on. Military life did not suit his dreamy
temperament. He was taunted by the 'louse-looking corporal'.
His resilience snapped on parade one morning; he attacked the
taunting corporal and only narrowly missed a severe punish-
ment.

When he returned to Helpston after eighteen months in the
militia, Clare again had ideas of courting his Mary. His hopes
were dashed and his amorous proposals were, it would seem,
rejected, and Mary was to die a spinster.

He became a lime burner at a neighbouring village and it
was here he met Martha Turner, 'Patty of the Vale'. She was the
daughter of a smallholder and came to live with the Clares at
Helpston. (A child was on the way and was to be followed by a
further seven.)

John Clare was continuing to write his verse, drawing on his
intimate knowledge of nature and country life. He made great
efforts to find a publisher and just before his marriage to Patty
he was successful. *Poems Descriptive of Rural Life and Scenery*
was accepted by John Taylor (who was also the publisher of

66

Badger

When midnight comes a host of dogs and men
Go out and track the badger to his den,
And put a sack within the hole, and lie
Till the old grunting badger passes by.
He comes and hears — they let the strongest loose.
The old fox hears the noise and drops the goose.
The poacher shoots and hurries from the cry,
And the old hare half wounded buzzes by.
They get a forked stick to bear him down
And clap the dogs and take him to the town,
And bait him all the day with many dogs,
And laugh and shout and fright the scampering hogs.
He runs along and bites at all he meets:
They shout and hollo down the noisy streets.

He turns about to face the loud uproar
And drives the rebels to their very door.
The frequent stone is hurled where'er they go;
When badgers fight, then every one's a foe.
The dogs are clapt and urged to join the fray;
The badger turns and drives them all away.
Though scarcely half as big, demure and small,
He fights with dogs for hours and beats them all.
The heavy mastiff, savage in the fray,
Lies down and licks his feet and turns away.
The bulldog knows his match and waxes cold,
The badger grins and never leaves his hold.
He drives the crowd and follows at their heels
And bites them through — the drunkard swears and reels.

The frighted women take the boys away,
The blackguard laughs and hurries on the fray.
He tries to reach the woods, an awkward race,
But sticks and cudgels quickly stop the chase.
He turns agen and drives the noisy crowd
And beats the many dogs in noises loud.
He drives away and beats them every one,
And then they loose them all and set them on.
He falls as dead and kicked by boys and men,
Then starts and grins and drives the crowd agen;
Till kicked and torn and beaten out he lies
And leaves his hold and cackles, groans and dies.

JOHN CLARE

Keats' works). The book was an immediate success and liked by the London critics. He journeyed to the City and met many eminent literary figures, but in his village he was isolated and lonely. There was, however, little real money in writing. Clare considered returning to farm work but labour required on the enclosed land was diminishing and he decided to persevere with his poetry.

There were two further published books of verse, *The Village Minstrel* in 1821 and the now celebrated *The Shepherd's Calendar* in 1827, but neither was popular with the public whose taste was turning from rural studies. *The Rural Muse* failed dismally.

One can imagine with little money coming into the household that relations between Clare and Patty deteriorated. However, in 1832, although John was reluctant, the family moved to a more comfortable cottage three miles away from Helpston at Northborough.

Clare's mental state was now suspect. He imagined that he had been married before — to his first love, Mary. He entered a private asylum in Epping Forest, the fees being settled by his friends. He studied in the surround of woods, gardens and fields during his four years' residence. When he left the asylum, he walked the eighty miles home to Northborough. He was, however, obviously still ill as he wrote that he 'returned home out of Essex and found no Mary; her and her family are nothing to me now though she was once the dearest of all . . .' He suffered from hallucinatory thoughts (such as imagining he was Wellington or Napoleon or Byron or even Shakespeare) and fits. But he continued to write magnificent and deeply perceptive verse.

John Clare was certified insane in December 1841, and was forcibly removed to the County Lunatic Asylum at Northampton. He was then forty-nine and was to spend the rest of his life there. During the twenty-three years in the asylum, Clare was encouraged to continue to write. He sighed for his liberty, he sighed for his loves, there is sadness in his poems. But often there was a simple and poignant sincerity, especially when he found solace in nature, be it 'The Red Robin', or 'Little Trotty Wagtail', or 'The Daisy' ('a happy flower'), or 'The Violet'. John Clare died in Northampton Asylum on 20 May 1864.

The Vixen

Among the taller wood with ivy hung,
The old fox plays and dances round her young,
She snuffs and barks if any passes by
And swings her tail and turns prepared to fly,
The horseman hurries by, she bolts to see,
And turns agen, from danger never free.
If any stands she runs among the poles
And barks and snaps and drives them in the holes.
The shepherd sees them and the boy goes by
And gets a stick and progs the hole to try.
They get all still and lie in safety sure,
And out again when everything's secure,
And start and snap at blackbirds bouncing by
To fight and catch the great white butterfly.

JOHN CLARE

69

John Clare Walk

1. From the centre of Helpston *(Clare's grave is in the churchyard)* cross the B1443 by the Clare monument and fourteenth-century cross.

2. Walk down Woodgate past the Blue Bell Inn *(where Clare worked)*, and Clare's cottage *(his birthplace)*.

3. At the junction turn right (Broad Wheel Road).

4. Turn left at a T-junction and walk down the Roman road. *Roman relics have been found in the area and John Clare uncovered a fine mosaic pavement.*

5. Opposite the corner of the wood turn left (unsigned footpath). Keep by the hedge and brook.

6. Cross the ditch by a plank bridge. Keep ahead (the woods are now away to the left) to the lane at Snip Green *(called Sneap Green in a Clare poem)*.

7. Turn left for 200 yards. At a bend turn right down a farm track (no cars sign).

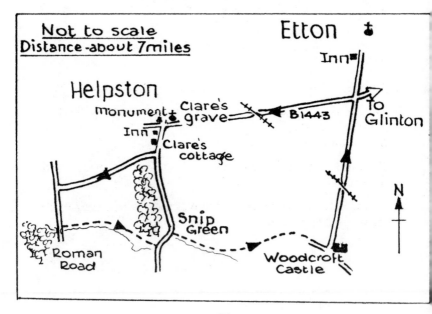

The John Clare Memorial, Helpston

8 The track now borders a brook; keep ahead at a junction.

9 The track becomes a lane to the junction by thirteenth-century Woodcroft Castle *(where Clare worked for the Bellair family).*

10 Turn left and cross the railway to the B1443. Etton is over the crossroads *(a pretty village and inn).*

11 Retrace steps to the B1443. Follow this road over the level-crossing to Helpston.

Like most writers George Eliot (born Mary Ann Evans) used her own experiences as the framework on which to build her tales.

Many of George Eliot's novels are set in North Warwickshire, rather flat, heavy farmland over which towns are slowly nibbling their way. There are many places which with thinly disguised names are recognised as being described in books such as *Silas Marner, Adam Bede, The Mill on the Floss, Scenes from Clerical Life* and *Middlemarch*.

Although most of her writing was done elsewhere, she drew on her knowledge of country life and country folk and recalled with a clear perception anecdotes and local gossip garnered during her early life.

Robert Evans, George Eliot's father, was born in 1773. He was a carpenter like his father and set up his own business in Ellastone, Staffordshire, in a big house called Wootton Hall, which was let to Francis Parker. (Many of the buildings were to be recalled later and used in *Adam Bede*.)

Through a friendship with the son of Francis Parker, Robert secured the post of forester, then head bailiff. He was obviously a born manager although not particularly literate. In 1801 he married Harriet, a girl who worked at the Hall.

When Francis Parker inherited the Newdigate estate, Kirk Hallam, Robert Evans moved to manage the lands; by this time there were two Evans children and Robert also had a farm of his own at Kirk Hallam.

The head of the Parker-Newdigate family, Sir Roger Newdigate, had seats at Harefield, Middlesex, and Arbury Hall, near Nuneaton, Warwickshire. By his will he left the estates to Francis Parker-Newdigate for life. In about 1804, a few years before Sir Roger's death, Francis and his wife took over the Gothic-style Arbury Hall. (This was renamed Cheverel Manor, the home of Sir Christopher Cheverel, by George Eliot in *Mr. Gilfil's Love-Story*.)

Again Francis sent for Robert Evans and the family moved to Arbury Farm (called South Farm today). Within five years Robert's wife died and was buried in Astley churchyard, near Astley Castle. (The castle was Knebley Abbey, the home of the Oldinports in *Mr. Gilfil's Love-Story*.)

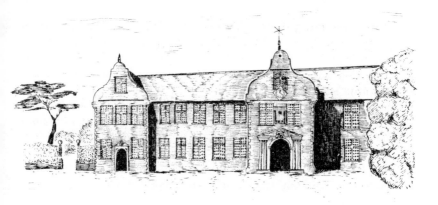

Arbury Hall Stables

In 1813 Robert married again; Christina, then aged twenty-five, was from a modestly wealthy family from farming stock. Mary Ann was their child, born on 22 November 1819.

A few months after her birth the family moved to another estate property, Griff House, which was larger than Arbury Farm. Many settings around Griff House feature in *The Mill on the Floss*. It was here that Philip Wakem met Maggie Tulliver.

Mary Ann was her father's favourite and would often be taken to the Hall and into the farmlands in the gig. She was an accomplished pianist from an early age; like the other Evans children Mary Ann was to be given a sound education. She attended with her brother Isaac (to whom she was very attached) the Dame School run by Mrs Moore near Griff House.

Christina Evans had two more children: twin boys William and Thomas, but they only survived ten days. Not in good health, Mrs Evans sent Mary Ann to her Aunt Evarard where she joined her sister Chrissey at Miss Lathom's school. Mary Ann was still only five and in the spartan house she became very homesick. She pined for the holidays back at Griff House and to be reunited with Isaac. She was not an attractive child and was said to be very clumsy. In her loneliness Mary Ann, although slow to start, became an avid reader. The girl particularly had a liking for Sir Walter Scott's novels, then much in vogue.

After four years with Miss Lathom the Evanses moved Mary Ann to a school in Nuneaton. In Church Lane there was a small boarding school, The Elms, owned by Mrs Wallington with Maria Lewis as governess. Miss Lewis was a very strict

Christian and greatly influenced the young girl from a rather easy-going family. Mrs Wallington stimulated Mary Ann's desire to learn; she responded and by the age of thirteen it was thought that Mrs Wallington could teach her little more and another school was sought.

The Misses Franklin's school was in the city of Coventry — in the 'best' part. Nantglyn gave a good but severe education and Mary Ann excelled at French, music and English composition. She left school in 1835.

The following year her father was very ill but it was her mother Christina, never in good health, who died in the February.

Chrissey and Mary Ann Evans kept house for their father and in the evenings Mary Ann read the novels of Sir Walter Scott to him as her mother had done. When her sister married, Mary Ann, with the aid of servants, looked after her father. She still possessed the Evangelical fervour which was instilled at school, and she refused to go to the theatre with her brother and devoted long periods to the reading of theology. She could visit the well-stocked library of Arbury Hall to further her excursions into the literary world.

Her first published work was a religious poem in the *Christian Observer* dated January 1840.

In 1841 Robert Evans, almost seventy and at the end of his working life, moved to a rather grand house at Foleshill, Coventry. Mary Ann continued to read avidly, with Wordsworth an especial favourite author; religious tracts were also always in evidence.

In November 1841 she met Charles Bray, then thirty and a free-thinker on religious matters. Her life suddenly took a different turn. She stopped going to church which caused much anxiety to her father. The subsequent break with Robert Evans was soon healed but Mary Ann was only outwardly a church-going believer again. Her beloved father died in 1849 and within days Charles Bray took Mary Ann for a continental holiday.

Now calling herself Marian, she moved to London and in a bookshop first made acquaintance with George Henry Lewes, a minor author and married with four sons. His unfaithful wife was Agnes. The friendship between Lewes and Marian blossomed and in the summer of 1854 they went to Weimar in Germany, then on to Berlin.

South Farm

Lewes and Marian were to return to England the following year and they settled in Richmond, Surrey. Marian wrote articles and essays for the *Westminster and Fortnightly Review.* She had not at first informed her family of her cohabitation with Lewes. When she did her brothers and sisters broke off relations with her.

In the summer of 1856, after some prompting from Lewes, she started her first major work, *The Sad Fortunes of the Reverend Amos Burton.* She wrote 'that it is a composition which I hope to make one of a series called "Scenes of Clerical Life".'

Early next year she informed her publisher Blackwood that her pseudonym would be George Eliot. The acceptance by the general public of an authoress in the last century was difficult. It was said that George was used as it was Lewes' name and Eliot 'because it was a good mouth-filling easily-pronounced word'.

The book of *Amos Barton* was well received by literary critics, but caused a stir in Marian's Warwickshire where the places and people described were recognised with some distaste. The identity of the author, however, was still shrouded in mystery.

In 1859 *Adam Bede* appeared. 'It will be a country story', Marian had indicated, 'full of the breath of cows and the scent of hay.' The book was an instant success but when the author's name was disclosed there was much condemnation of Marian's private life. This was increased in her old home countryside; so many situations and characters were featured — not even her father, Robert Evans, escaped, who was Adam Bede.

In the same year that *Adam Bede* was published Marian gave birth to a son, Charles, but this does not appear to have diminished her literary output as in 1860 came *The Mill on the Floss*. The book was perhaps her most popular novel but the initial reviews were mixed. Some objected to the immorality. Again in this work there were many associations with Marian's former life, with the Maggie of the story being the young Mary Evans; her brother Isaac was Tom and there were many settings recalled from childhood memories. However, Marian, although having much fame and acclamation, continued to be socially unacceptable.

In 1861 the new book was *Silas Marner*, my personal favourite. This was popular with the reading public because of its moral correctness and evokes the spirit of the Midland shires of Victorian times with its rural and hunting connotations and strict class structure.

The output continued with *Romola*, Marian's first novel that was not set in England. Although Marian and Lewes continued to be based in London they often spent long periods on the continent, and they were especially fond of Italy. In 1863 they moved to a newly built house, The Priory, near the Regent's Park Canal.

Felix Holt was begun in 1865 and took fourteen months to finish. Marian then turned to poetry and this occupied her for the next three years with Wordsworth her inspiration. Some of her poetical works (for example 'Brother and Sister') were autobiographical although her break with her relations was almost complete. Little attempt was made to heal the rift.

The first part of *Middlemarch* appeared in December 1871 at a price of five shillings. It was to be a four-part work and again there were identifications with Warwickshire folk.

With financial security and literary success Marian began to be acceptable to society. In her turn she became more conventional. She met the Queen's children and it was said the monarch admired her work.

Two Lovers

Two lovers by a moss-grown spring:
   They leaned soft cheeks together there.
   Mingled the dark and sunny hair,
And heard the wooing thrushes sing.
        O budding time!
        O love's blest prime!

Two wedded from the portal stept:
   The bells made happy carollings,
   The air was soft as fanning wings,
   White petals on the pathway slept.
        O pure-eyed bride!
        O tender pride!

Two faces o'er a cradle bent:
   Two hands above the head were locked;
   These pressed each other while they rocked,
Those watched a life that love had sent.
        O solemn hour!
        O hidden power!

Two parents by the evening fire:
   The red light fell about their knees
   On heads that rose by slow degrees
   Like buds upon the lily spire,
        O patient life!
        O tender strife!

The two still sat together there,
   The red light shone about their knees;
   But all the heads by slow degrees
   Had gone and left that lonely pair,
        O voyage fast!
        O vanished past!

The red light shone upon the floor
   And made the space between them wide;
   They drew their chairs up side by side,
Their pale cheeks joined, and said, 'Once more!'
        O memories!
        O past that is!   GEORGE ELIOT

Marian's plot for *Daniel Deronda* was conceived while the Leweses were on holiday in Germany; they saw young women in the grasp of wicked men. However, the gestation was to be some years and the book did not appear until 1876. Marian at last did not need to draw on the experiences of her long-ago past in the Midlands or base characterisation on old friends and relations.

Her health began to deteriorate and there was the need of restful holidays and a country house. With the help of a young friend, Johnny Cross, they found The Heights, a large red-brick mansion set in eight acres of magnificent grounds near Haslemere in Surrey.

For Marian and Lewes time together at The Heights was to prove short for in 1878 George Lewes died. With her great distress Marian could not even bear to attend the funeral.

She was consoled by Johnny Cross, who had also just suffered a bereavement — that of his mother. With anything but Victorian correctness, Marian and Cross were in love by the summer of 1879. The following year they married and journeyed to Venice for the honeymoon, but within a few months she was very ill with a kidney infection. The marriage was to last little more than six months; on 22 December 1880 George Eliot died. She was buried in a grave in unconsecrated ground in London's Highgate Cemetery.

Sweet Evenings Come and Go, Love

'La noche buena se viene,
  La noche buena se va,
Y nosotros nos iremos
  Y no volveremos más.

Sweet evenings come and go, love,
  They came and went of yore:
This evening of our life, love,
  Shall go and come no more.

When we have passed away, love,
  All things will keep their name;
But yet no life on earth, love,
  With ours will be the same.

The daisies will be there, love,
  The stars in heaven will shine:
I shall not feel they wish, love,
  Nor thou my hand in thine.

A better time will come, love,
  And better souls be born:
I would not be the best, love,
  To leave thee now forlorn.

GEORGE ELIOT

George Eliot Walk

1 The starting place is the village of Astley (*Knebley*). *George Eliot's parents were married in the church.*

2 Walk along the B4102 towards Nuneaton. Go by Seaswood Pool *(once a canal feeder lake).*

3 Just over the bridge turn right to climb a double stile. Keep at the side of the field.

4 Go through the drive of Arbury Park (*Cheverel Manor — George Eliot's father was land agent here*).

5 Cross the drive and field to a fenced track. Walk along the road near a school.

6 Turn right (the sign is broken) on a wide farm track.

7 As the farm track bends sharp left towards the farm keep on the old heading (there is a hedge on the left) for 100 yards.

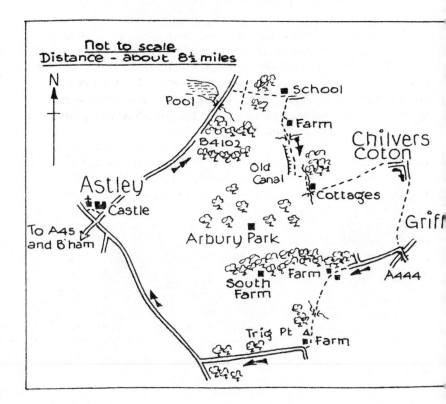

Astley Church

8　Bear left (the hedge is now on the right). Go through a rough area and follow the edge of a hollyhedge to climb a step stile.

9　Bear right to cross a brook. Continue on to a bank (side of an old canal). Turn left for ½ mile at the edge of the field.

10　Strike out over the field to the left to a coppice. Turn right to keep at the side of the wood and stream to the farm road.

11　Turn left and stay on the road to the houses at Chilvers Coton. Turn right. At the end of the road keep ahead over rough land to a lane.

12　By the main road to the left is Griff House. *George Eliot lived here with her parents from 1820 to 1841.*

13　Turn right on the lane. When the lane bears right keep straight on then left of the gates to Arbury Park.

14　At a muddy farmyard turn left. Continue on the left side of the hedge. Cross a footbridge and go over a stile. (To the right is South Farm — *George Eliot's birthplace.*)

15　Past a trig point bear right to a lane. Keep ahead to the T-junction. Turn right to Astley.

Nudging Puddletown Forest, at Higher Bockhampton, three miles from Dorchester, is the thatch-roofed cottage where Thomas Hardy was born on 2 June 1840. The cottage was built by the writer's great-grandfather who sited the place on what was then a very isolated spot on the western fringes of Egdon Heath. Hardy called the heathland 'untameable' — it has now been tamed by the Forestry Commission.

Hardy's grandfather and father carried on the family building business from the cottage at Bockhampton, using part of the house as an office. There were four children: Hardy's sisters Mary and Kate and his brother Henry, older by eleven years.

Before his marriage, Thomas Hardy's father, also Thomas, was reckoned to have a great liking for the girls of the village, and it was said he got some into trouble. With Jemima Hand, who worked as a housemaid, there was no escape; when she was three months' pregnant she married Hardy. It was not thought that their baby Thomas would live as he was very delicate.

From an early age young Thomas developed a love of music and folk song. The family was musical too; Hardy's father played in the church orchestra at Stinsford — the building so lovingly described in the village of Mellstock in *Under the Greenwood Tree*. The musicians were placed in the gallery and the young Hardy, playing the violin, was to join his father, his uncle and grandfather. Not far away from the church is the magnificent mansion where the lady befriended Thomas Hardy. Mrs Martin had no children of her own and became passionately fond of the young Hardy, almost from his infancy. He was to use the place as a setting for *Desperate Remedies*. Thomas Hardy, senior was in great demand as a player for country dances and the young Thomas was given an accordion by his father for his fourth birthday.

A new school was opened in Lower Bockhampton and in 1848 the boy was one of the first pupils. Thomas' second school was governed by the British and Foreign School Society, a nonconformist group, in Dorchester. It had a good reputation for scholarly education.

Sunday walks with his parents were a regular feature for the young Hardy. They tramped across the heath to the silent pool called Rushy Pond and over the heights of the Rainbarrows. Hardy's father would point out local landmarks; his mother told of local legend and folklore. Hardy took an interest in a subject that was to abide all his life — the study of nature.

On his journeys to Dorchester he was in a new world. The railway had just arrived, bringing with it prosperity. There were the army barracks and conflict was common in the town; the assizes were sited here, with its prisoners and hangings. Hardy witnessed the cock fights and the anti-Catholic displays, scenes that were to be inscribed on his memory.

Hardy's school was run by Mr Isaac Last who was strict but sound. Being such a good reader, and encouraged by his ambitious mother, Hardy advanced well. When he was thirteen he transferred with his teacher to Mr Last's new fee-paying school. This was fortuitous as he could now continue beyond the normal school-leaving age. He learnt French and Latin but

Hardy's Cottage

83

does not appear to have been particularly interested in creative literature.

With the age of sixteen nearing, a career had to be chosen. Hardy's father thought of the Church. However, when Hardy, senior met an architect on a restoration job it was suggested that his son might be taken on as an articled apprentice with the architect, John Hicks of Dorchester.

Hardy started at the South Street premises a month after he was sixteen; his employer encouraged his workers to read and study. Hardy's first published piece was a skit about a clock and appeared in the local paper. He continued by writing anonymously about restorations being undertaken by John Hicks.

Hardy witnessed the public hanging of a woman in 1856; the young man was far from being appalled and this was another scene that was to be used later in *Tess of the D'Urbervilles*. He described his life at this time as 'a life twisted of three strands — the professional life, the scholar's life and the rustic life.'

Hardy's paternal grandmother, who had been such an encouragement to his progress, died in 1857. His new influence was Horatio (Horace) Moule, the son of a clergyman who dabbled in poetry, who urged Hardy to try his hand at this style of literature.

Stinsford Church

He renewed his apprenticeship with Hicks while considering his next path, which was to be a move to lodgings in London in April 1862; he secured a post with Mr Blomfield. Hardy especially enjoyed the musical and artistic life in London and was enthusiastic about opera, and practised well-known arias on the fiddle.

Hardy read avidly but found London life, although stimulating, rather monotonous. He especially missed his friends and relations back home in Dorset. In 1865, he had a humorous piece accepted for publication in *Chamber's Journal.* It was composed in Blomfield's office to amuse the young students. He also wrote some poetry and thought of writing plays in blank verse; to obtain first-hand experience, he secured a walk-on part in a play at Covent Garden.

After repeated efforts for two years, Hardy could find no takers for the poems and the pressures of the London years almost caused a breakdown in his health. It was fortuitous that his old employer, John Hicks, was also far from well in 1867 and was looking for an assistant. In July, Hardy returned to Bockhampton. The daily routine of walking to the Dorchester office restored his health and, in August, he began to write a novel.

By the middle of January the following year, the first draft of *The Poor Man and the Lady* was complete. Some of the plot for the story was undoubtedly autobiographical. The work was put into shape within a further five months and sent to his friend Horace Moule for his opinion. The result was a letter of introduction from Moule to the publisher, Alexander Macmillan. The firm did not accept or reject the manuscript but advised either rewriting or the submission of another novel.

His architectural work took Hardy to Weymouth and he resumed writing verses but soon he was to start the new novel *Desperate Remedies,* using local knowledge and experiences. He did not make the book essentially a rural tale but rather melodrama and wrote at a speedy pace. On returning to the family house at Bockhampton, he continued the writing and it was all but finished by March 1870. The manuscript was duly sent to Macmillan and, awaiting the answer, he could barely concentrate on the church-building commissions. Hardy was sent to St Juliot near Boscastle, Cornwall, to advise on the restoration of a decaying church. He was met by the rector's sister-in-law, Emma Lavinia Gifford, and immediately fell in love with her.

On Hardy's return to Dorset, a letter of rejection from Macmillan arrived — the publishers did not want *Desperate Remedies*. Undismayed, he submitted it to William Tinsley; subject to alterations and the payment of £75 towards expenses, conditions which Hardy accepted with alacrity, the book was accepted for publication.

In August 1870, Hardy again visited Cornwall and the initial first love blossomed. He took Emma on long walks and picnics, when they read poetry and talked of literature.

The book (published anonymously) received mixed reviews. While the country life portrayed was praised, the story was termed 'unpleasant'. Undeterred, Hardy speeded along his new work. Called originally *The Mellstock Quire*, it was later retitled *Under the Greenwood Tree*. The work was firmly set in his home county.

Desperate Remedies had lost money, both for Hardy and the publishers. However, Tinsley purchased the copyright of the new manuscript for £40 and the book appeared in 1872. *A Pair of Blue Eyes*, placed in Cornwall with local characters and incidents, was serialised by the same publisher for Hardy's fee of £200.

Hardy, still not writing under his own name, was introduced to the leading man of letters of the time, Leslie Stephen, editor of the *Cornhill Magazine*. This journal featured serialised works of good fiction. Hardy accepted Stephen's offer to purchase his next work. It would be a rural tale called *Far From the Madding Crowd*.

The suicide of his friend Horace Moule heightened the pathos and feeling in the new pastoral work that so evokes the scenery of Dorset. When the first chapters appeared, it was suggested the author might be George Eliot. Popularity in America followed and Hardy now thought able to take the steps to marriage.

On 17 September 1874, he married Emma Gifford at Paddington; none of Hardy's relations attended the ceremony — it was a wedding between a self-taught rural man and a sophisticated middle-class lady and did not auger well.

The instalments of *Far From the Madding Crowd* were highly praised and appeared in book form in November. Sales were very brisk and Emma was happy to be married to a successful novelist, albeit one from humble roots. *The Hand of Ethelberta* — again serialised — was a disappointment to publishers, critics, the public and, perhaps most of all, to Emma. During the next few years, Hardy and Emma lived in London, Yeovil and Sturminster Newton, where *The Return of the Native* was written. Although now away from Bockhampton, he again set a novel on his homeland heath where he roamed in his youth. In fact, it has been said that the heath, with a whole chapter devoted to it, is the main character; here, Hardy is recalling his childhood on the wild expanse.

There was now a lack of contact between Hardy and his old parental home, as though a gulf had developed between his background and upbringing and his new life married to the daughter of a solicitor. Emma was never taken into his family's confidence and remained an outsider.

Hardy worked next on *The Trumpet Major*, which was published in 1880 and admired by the critics. By now he had moved back to London and turned his back on his native countryside. But the Hardys were soon to return to Dorset, first to Wimborne, where *Two on a Tower* was produced; a move

Max Gate

87

was then made to Dorchester. For *The Mayor of Casterbridge* Hardy could draw on the local setting, its history and its rustic characters. Many anecdotes, told to Hardy by his mother, were recalled.

The author, turning his hand to his old profession, designed a nondescript and cold house, called Max Gate, on a site on the outskirts of Dorchester. Coming back to his old territory permanently was a conscious effort to go back to his pastoral roots and away from the sophisticated life. Although Hardy enjoyed the new bicycling craze with Emma, touring far into the countryside of his Wessex, there was little sign of affection between the two. Hardy's philandering with other women did not help. Also, he was cut off from his Dorset relatives. Emma found an escape in narrow religious views, while Hardy had lost his faith. His books now painted a depressing rather than an optimistic picture; he tried to lose his rural past and present himself as a middle-class man of letters.

At Max Gate he wrote *The Woodlanders* (1887), *Tess of the D'Urbervilles* (1891), *The Well-Beloved* (serialised in *The Illustrated News* in 1892) and *Jude the Obscure* (1895).

Tess, perhaps based on the life-story of the favourite grandmother, gave Hardy a confidence and financial security to attack the conventions of the cosy society which he had come to dislike. The down-trodden Jude in *Jude the Obscure* turns to thoughts of unbelief and anti-marriage. Emma's reaction to *Jude the Obscure* was the predictable shock, especially as she was aware of her husband's infatuation at the time with other ladies.

From 1890, Hardy returned to his love of poetry; this move was given impetus by the poor reception *Jude the Obscure* received. He felt, too, that he had used up his powers as a novelist. In 1898, Hardy's first book of verse *Wessex Poems* was published. He tried unsuccessfully to placate his wife by stating that the poems were personal. *The Dynasts,* a dramatic verse written over many years and based on the Napoleonic war, was ended on an optimistic note for mankind when the last of the three parts was published in 1908. (He was to regret the final optimism when the First World War started.) *The Dynasts* was hailed as a masterpiece and Hardy, already acclaimed as a novelist, had really arrived as a great poet.

Hardy met Florence Emily Dugdale, who was to be the second Mrs Hardy, in 1907. She was twenty-eight and the

The Fallow Deer at the Lonely House

One without looks in tonight
   Through the curtain-chink
From the sheet of glistening white;
One without looks in tonight
   As we sit and think
   By the fender-brink.

We do not discern those eyes
   Watching in the snow;
Lit by lamps of rosy dyes
We do not discern those eyes
   Wondering, aglow,
   Fourfooted, tiptoe.

THOMAS HARDY

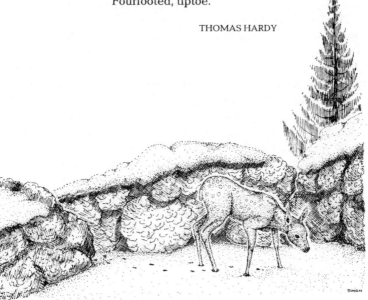

daughter of a teacher from a humble background. Florence, too, became a teacher, but aspired to be a creative writer. Emma and Thomas Hardy were both seventy in 1910. Emma's health was failing and she could not attend the presentation of the Order of Merit to her husband. The same year, Dorchester bestowed on Hardy the freedom of the town — both Emma Hardy and Florence Dugdale were in attendance.

Two years later, Emma was dead; within a month Florence was living at Max Gate and, in February 1914, she and Hardy became Mr and Mrs Hardy at a ceremony in Enfield parish church. Hardy was soon to be smitten by remorse with many fine verses recalling times spent with Emma. Over fifty poems were written in two years, expressing sentiments which must have pained his new love, who was, in any case, of poor stature and health. The obsession of Hardy for things past included visits to places like Cornwall, where Emma and Hardy fell in love.

By the summer, war broke out; Hardy was shattered and despaired for the future of mankind. He was now very wealthy but he kept Florence short of money; it is said she had to supplement the housekeeping account from her dress allowance; she paid for an operation from her own private income.

The writer's output of poems continued, still reminiscent and often recalling the local countryside and nature. Towards the end of the war, Hardy decided that a record of his life, purged of any indiscretions, should be completed. After a brief abortive attempt in which Hardy assisted Florence to write the life, he decided to start again. This time Hardy would do the actual composition but the work would be written in the third person under his wife's name. Rough notes, correspondence and diaries used in the so-called biography were destroyed immediately after each part of the manuscript was finished.

At the same time, Hardy found many verses composed years ago and also penned new poetry for fresh books. He would visit his old haunts, including the Bockhampton cottage. This gave the inspiration for 'The Fallow Deer at the Lonely House'.

On 11 December 1927, Hardy took to his bed, complaining of being tired; a month later, on 11 January 1928, the weakly baby, not expected to survive, died, aged eighty-seven. He was buried in Westminster Abbey and his heart was buried in Stinsford.

The Faithful Swallow

When summer shone
Its sweetest on
An August day,
'Here evermore,'
I said, 'I'll stay;
Not go away
To another shore
As fickle they!'

December came;
'Twas not the same!
I did not know
Fidelity
Would serve me so.
Frost, hunger, snow;
And now, ah me,
Too late to go!

THOMAS HARDY

The Robin

When up aloft
I fly and fly,
I see in pools
The shining sky,
And a happy bird
Am I, am I!

When I descend
Towards their brink
I stand, and look,
And stoop, and drink,
And bathe my wings,
And chink and prink.

When winter frost
Makes earth as steel
I search and search
But find no meal,
And most unhappy
Then I feel.

But when it lasts,
And snows still fall,
I get to feel
No grief at all,
For I turn to a cold stiff
Feathery ball!

THOMAS HARDY

91

Thomas Hardy Walk

1 The walk starts at the car park of Thorncombe Wood Nature Trails (off the A35 and Cuckoo Lane). Leaflets describing the nature trails are obtainable.

2 Follow the signs through the trees to Hardy's Cottage; you will pass the monument to Hardy 'from American friends'.

3 Go down the vehicle track to join the road. Turn left then right down a farm drive.

4 As the drive bends keep ahead through metal gates and ignore the stile.

5 Go through another metal gate and follow the direction of a right-hand waymark arrow. Climb the stile to a field.

6 Walk to the far top corner of the field. Go over a stile to join a lane. Turn right past the gates of Kingston Maurward.

7 Turn left down a lane to Stinsford and the church. *Hardy family graves.*

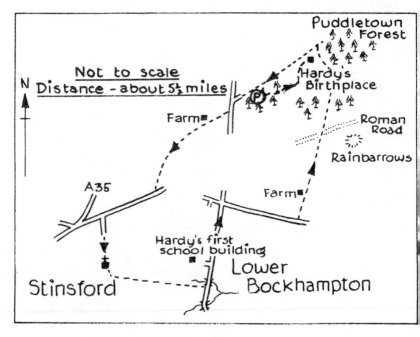

8 Proceed along a wide track that borders the tributary of the River Frome. At a lane turn left to Lower Bockhampton. *Hardy's school.*

9 At the crossroads turn right for ½ mile. Climb the hill and proceed left down the drive of Pine Lodge Farm.

10 Go through a metal gate past the buildings. Keep ahead by a hedge.

11 By the pool pass through a gate. *'Rainbarrows' are to the right.* Cross the Roman road to Hardy's Cottage.

12 Walk along the previous vehicle track to the car park.

A. E. Housman — Alfred Edward Housman — wrote so much about Shropshire that it is a little surprising to find that he did not ever live in the county for any length of time. In his childhood, he would roam to the top of a hill (his Mount Pisgah) near Bromsgrove in Worcestershire, and set eyes on the far distance with the Shropshire Hills of the Long Mynd, Wenlock Edge and The Wrekin on the horizon. The poetic memories in later years were a pining nostalgia for the Midland countryside, while the Professor Housman lived in Cambridge or London.

Alfred's grandfather was a parson and moved with his family to Catshill, near Bromsgrove. Alfred's father, Edward, was the second son and like his younger brother loved the country life and sports. He was encouraged by his great uncle, John Adams, of nearby Perry Hall, to be a solicitor. (On the death of the uncle, Edward was to become life tenant of Perry Hall.) Through a friendship with a cousin, Edward met Sarah Williams, the daughter of a parson. After their marriage in 1858 they moved to Fockbury and within a year their son was born and was christened Alfred Edward by his grandfather.

The great uncle at Perry Hall died when Alfred was only a few months old, so the family moved into this grand house on the outskirts of Bromsgrove. There were six further Housman children and they had a splendid play place in the grounds of Perry Hall. They were talented youngsters and with their mother's background had a sound religious instruction. They were comfortably off, both from Edward Housman's legal post and from inherited wealth.

Sadness, however, was soon to strike the family. In 1869 Mrs Housman was found to have cancer and her condition gradually worsened. Finance for the large family was now in shorter supply but Edward had the hope to send his son Alfred to his old school, King Edward's, Bromsgrove.

He was able to do so only by Alfred gaining one of the free 'foundation scholar' places in 1870. When Mrs Housman's health worsened, Alfred, praying intently for his mother to get better, was sent to friends at Woodchester. While still there — on his twelfth birthday — his mother died and within a few months he had turned his back on Christianity.

Remains of The Clock House

The family moved to Fockbury House (called The Clock House) and Mr Housman's cousin, Mary, came to look after the children. In 1873 Edward and Mary's sister, Lucy, married.

Alfred developed a talent for verse at school. He also loved to walk; he viewed the countryside from the hilltops with his eyes often turning westwards to the Shropshire that he was to write about in later years with such affection.

About 1875, when Alfred was sixteen or so, he produced a family magazine, getting his brothers and sisters to contribute. The magazine was circulated among his relations and friends. Poetry continued to be the boy's forte and he won the verse prize again at Bromsgrove School.

His father, Edward, was not a good manager of his financial affairs and money began to be short; debtors started to press and Edward turned more and more to drink. His health began to suffer.

Alfred in turn became depressed and quiet. His verse was on melancholic subjects, death and sadness, but his school work does not seem to have suffered and his success in classical studies was especially noticed. He was appointed head boy in 1877. Still he loved country walks and still he gazed across Worcestershire to Wenlock Edge and the Shropshire Hills.

In June 1877 he heard that he had won a scholarship to St John's College, Oxford, to read classics. The award was just in time, for in the summer his father was forced to sell Fockbury House and return to Perry Hall on the outskirts of Bromsgrove.

Alfred was at first an assiduous and conscientious student and contributed widely to literary magazines. He discovered the beauty of the Oxfordshire countryside and went on many long walking excursions, and he developed an especial friendship for another student, the scientist Moses Jackson. Alfred's devotion to study began to waver. He became somewhat over-confident and at odds with his tutors, especially with his philosophy professor.

When he was about to take his finals, his father suffered a severe stroke. Added to the lack of concentrated work, Alfred was ill-prepared to sit the degree examination and the result

Perry Hall, Bromsgrove

was absolute failure. Edward's health gradually improved but with the family finances stretched, Alfred only returned to Oxford to collect his belongings and turned instead to the Civil Service. He studied for the entrance examination (and at the same time the retake of the Oxford degree). He was successful in both and for the next six years worked in London with his friend Moses Jackson at the Patent Office.

Alfred was to realise that he was in love with Moses Jackson — an ardent love that he was to know was not reciprocated. His anguish was increased by the fact that although he was by now an atheist, he still upheld the teachings of the Church and remembered that to be homosexual was considered sinful.

He went on walks alone; it was on these excursions over Hampstead Heath that he would find the inspiration for verse. He put his poems in an old notebook that he had used as reference for his classical studies and by 1892 Housman had composed eighty pages of verse. There was no intention at this time to publish them. The inspiration was nostalgia for the past days. He recalled the views and images of his Worcestershire and the Shropshire Hills in the distance from Bromsgrove:

> Into my heart an air that kills
> From you far country blows:
> What are those
> blue remembered hills
> What spires, what farms
> are those?

With the imminent departure of Moses Jackson to India Alfred resumed his studies of the classics. He gained a good reputation and in 1892 secured the post of Professor of Latin at University College, London, where he was to remain for nineteen years. He was, in his own words, 'rescued from the gutter'.

His idea of a series of poems based on a Shropshire boy living in London and reminiscing about his home country ('on western horizons'), its characters and countryside fired his literary mind. He could express his own views, taking the part of the Shropshire lad and enthusiastically worked on the verses with a view to publication.

With the death of Housman's father in 1894, the output of poetry — much of it conceived on the lonely walks — increased. It is likely that he had not visited Shropshire since his childhood

97

Catshill Church

days and the descriptions were perhaps merely his visionary pictures which were sometimes inaccurate.

The collection of sixty-three poems was offered to Macmillan under the title *The poems of Terence Hearsay* — Hearsay was Housman's 'mouthpiece'. The work was rejected and Housman agreed with another publisher, Kegan Paul, to pay the £30 himself for a printing of five hundred copies. These were published in 1896 as *A Shropshire Lad.*

A second edition was issued after two years by a different publisher, Grant Richards Limited; this time the costs were borne by the publisher. Further editions came out and the work was sold to a New York firm, John Lane. Composers found the verses eminently suitable for the addition of music and over fifty of his poems have been used. One, 'Loveliest of trees, the cherry', has ten settings.

For many years Housman refused to take royalties from the ever increasing sales of *A Shropshire Lad.* 'I am not a poet by trade,' he avered; 'I am a Professor of Latin.' However, he continued to compose verse on many subjects. When his younger brother Herbert was killed in the Boer War in 1901 the event was reflected in moving and sombre lines:

> The Wain upon the northern steep
> Descends and lifts away
> Oh I will sit me down and weep
> For bones in Africa.

In 1911 he was made Professor of Latin at Cambridge, with a Fellowship at Trinity College, and the same year he received an Honorary Fellowship at the college where he failed his degree, St John's, Oxford.

Last Poems was published in 1922. The reviews were good and the sales reflected the public's approval. The initial 4,000 copies were increased by 17,000 before the end of the year.

Later in the decade, in 1930, the Poet Laureate, Robert Bridges, died. It was thought that Housman might have received the crowning poetic honour but, in the event, John Masefield was chosen.

In 1935 Housman became ill and was told to reduce the length of his walks to conserve his strength. He stayed in a nursing home in Cambridge for some weeks. He fitfully recovered and viewed Shropshire for the last time from his beloved hill near Bromsgrove but died, aged seventy-seven, on 30 April 1936. He was cremated and his ashes were placed appropriately in the churchyard of a Shropshire church, at Ludlow.

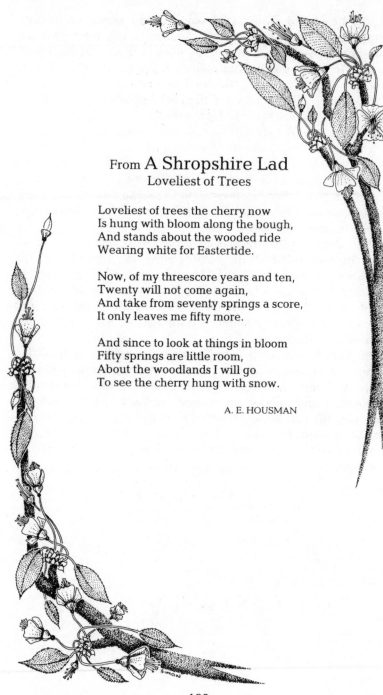

From A Shropshire Lad
Loveliest of Trees

Loveliest of trees the cherry now
Is hung with bloom along the bough,
And stands about the wooded ride
Wearing white for Eastertide.

Now, of my threescore years and ten,
Twenty will not come again,
And take from seventy springs a score,
It only leaves me fifty more.

And since to look at things in bloom
Fifty springs are little room,
About the woodlands I will go
To see the cherry hung with snow.

A. E. HOUSMAN

100

From A Shropshire Lad
When Smoke Stood up from Ludlow

When smoke stood up from Ludlow,
    And mist blew off from Teme,
And blithe afield to ploughing
    Against the morning beam
    I strode beside my team.

The blackbird in the coppice
    Looked out to see me stride,
And hearkened as I whistled
    The trampling team beside,
    And fluted and replied:

'Lie down, lie down, young yeoman;
    What use to rise and rise?'
Rise man a thousand mornings
    Yet down at last he lies,
    And then the man is wise.

I heard the tune he sang me,
    And spied his yellow bill;
I picked a stone and aimed it
    And threw it with a will:
    Then the bird was still.

Then my soul within me
    Took up the blackbird's strain,
And still beside the horses
    Along the dewy lane
    It sang the song again:

'Lie down, lie down, young yeoman;
    The sun moves always west;
The road one treads to labour
    Will lead one home to rest,
    And that will be the best.'

A. E. HOUSMAN

101

A. E. Housman Walk

1. From Bromsgrove go west along the A448 for ½ mile, passing Perry Hall.

2. Turn right (Willows Road) to a T-junction. Turn left (Crabtree Lane).

3. Opposite house no 115 go along a footpath to a lane. Turn right to a junction.

4. Turn left. Just before the motorway go down a ramp on the right. Follow the edge of the motorway for ½ mile. At the sign take the path to the right (Hinton Field).

5. At the B4091 turn left to Catshill church.

6. Retrace your steps along the B4091. By house no 417 go up a bank. A footpath leads to the motorway bridge.

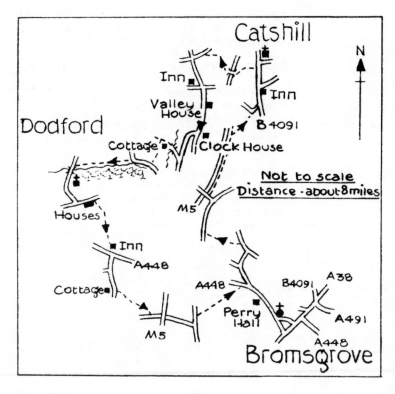

7 Take the track to a lane and turn left. At the junction turn left (Fairfield Road).

8 At the crossroads go over to Valley Road and pass Valley House *(another Housman home)* to The Clock House. *Housman lived nearby.*

9 Take the lane signed Dodford *(Chartist village and Priory)*. At the junction turn right (Brimstone Lane). Cross the brook.

10 Go to the right of the house. At once turn left to climb a bank to a meadow. Continue to the lane. Turn right for ¼ mile.

11 On a bend keep ahead through fields to a vehicle track and lane. Turn left to a T-junction.

12 Turn left then right over a stile at the end of the houses. Walk at the edges of the fields to the inn on the A448. Cross to the lane.

13 After ½ mile go over the stile opposite a cottage. In the pasture veer right to the corner gate. Keep by the right-hand hedge to a stile.

14 Aim for a white house. Climb the stile to a lane. Turn left and left again at the junction. Cross the brook and turn right by Echells Close.

15 Follow the footpath to the A448. Turn right for Bromsgrove.

The morning spread upon the mountains, beautiful Clyro rising from the valley and stretching away northward, dotted with white houses and shining with gleams of green on hills and dingle sides.

The writer is the Rev Francis Kilvert; the area he is describing so lovingly in his Diary is a mile or so north of Hay, where the Wye meanders a tranquil way through the foothills of the Welsh borderlands.

For almost ten years, from 18 January 1870 to 13 March 1879, Francis Kilvert kept a diary that has become an intuitive window on life in that period. After many years of intensive search, parts of the Diary remain missing. Some sections were destroyed by well-meaning folk to protect the wishes of past owners of the Diaries, or, in earlier years, entries were removed by those intimately involved or described. It is possible that some entries are closeted away and await discovery.

Kilvert was christened Robert Francis Kilvert, the second child of Robert and Thermuthis Kilvert. Like the other five children, Francis was born (1840) at Hardenhuish in Wiltshire where his father was vicar. The Rev Robert Kilvert, like many country parsons of the era, ran a school and the Kilvert children received their early formal education here. However, from about the age of eleven Francis Kilvert attended his learned uncle's school at Claverton Lodge on Bathwick Hill, Bath. The uncle (also Francis Kilvert) was a literary man with some of his works published and he no doubt instilled the love of poetry and literature into his pupils, including Francis.

In 1855 Robert Martyn Ashe, a cousin of Robert Kilvert's wife, became squire of Langley Burrell, a few miles from Hardenhuish. Although he was in Holy Orders himself he offered the living to the Rev Robert Kilvert.

The studious work of Francis Kilvert resulted in a place at Wadham College, Oxford. He read history and law from 1859. In 1862 he graduated (with a fourth) and in the following years was made a deacon (1863) and received Holy Orders (1864).

Kilvert was appointed as a curate in his father's parish but the same year journeyed to Clyro to be interviewed for a similar position. His friends and relations regarded his intention to settle in Radnorshire as a journey into exile. The Rev R. L. Venables was taken by the tall, black-bearded young man. Kilvert duly started his duties during the bitter winter weather of January 1865 and went into lodgings at Ashbrook House, Clyro, with Mrs Chaloner. The house still stands next to the village post office and stores, and opposite is the Baskerville Arms — the Swan Inn in Kilvert's day.

The countryside has changed little since the last century and today there are fine paths and ways across the valley through the Radnor Forest to the north and over the mountain foothills. We travel along the 'stony narrow green-banked lanes' on the walk. Kilvert was an inveterate walker and could easily cover twenty miles a day. He was a disciple of Wordsworth visiting many of the places the great poet visited. With a love of nature he could, in his Diary, describe with a perceptive eye the landscape of his travels. One of his favourite excursions was to Craig-Pwll-Du where the falls tumble down the rocks to the gorge of Bach Howey.

Ashbrook House, Clyro

We can trace on the Ordnance Survey map the line of the old Wye valley railway — the railway arrived just before Kilvert started his Diaries in Clyro. Needless to say, the line, perhaps one of the prettiest in the land with great tourist potential, has long been axed.

Although Francis Kilvert had composed poetry, the Diary was perhaps conceived as a New Year resolution in 1870. He had already been in Clyro for some five years and it has been suggested he decided to use some of his new-found spare time after the Rev Venables remarried. When Mr Venables was a widower Kilvert would spend many hours in his company, dining and discussing the affairs of the scattered parish and, when this facility was lost, Kilvert could jot down the happenings in his Diary notes.

Kilvert moved in a circle that was devoid of class consciousness; he could comment about the elite, the county landowners, the squire and the cottagers. One of the families was the Thomases. The Rev William Jones Thomas was vicar of Llanigon, near Hay. His youngest daughter, Daisy, and Kilvert were attracted to each other (so the diarist tells us) but opposition

Clyro Church

from the Rev Thomas (because of Kilvert's lowly position) killed any thoughts of marriage.

Kilvert in his Diary is not restricted to commenting on country matters. It is obvious from the record of his travels to London that he loved the theatre and art with visits to the galleries, concerts and pantomimes.

Back in the Clyro countryside the villaging (pastoral visiting) gave him a marvellous opportunity to observe the social scene and the plight of parishioners. The walks to the mountains and hills gave great scope to his talents as a descriptive writer —

> the mountains were silent and desolate. No human being in sight, not a tree, no living thing moving except a few mountain sheep, some of them with long curling horns . . . The only sounds were the sighing and the rushing of distant streams in the watercourses with which the mountain sides were seamed and scarred . . .

In 1872, influenced by the deafness of his father or the end of the romance with Daisy Thomas, Kilvert decided to resign from the post of curate of Clyro. He accepted the curacy of Langley Burrell again and from September 1872 served that parish for a few years.

Romance again blossomed while he lived at Langley Burrell. Kilvert met Katherine Heanley (called Kathleen Mavoureen by Kilvert) at a wedding at Findon in 1874 on the Downs above Worthing — he was groomsman and Kathleen a bridesmaid. It was love at first sight and the meetings and exchange of letters continued well into the following year. It was when he met the strikingly beautiful Etty Meredith Brown that the romance with Kathleen cooled. Unfortunately we will probably never be told the story of the secret courtship and his subsequent banishment from Etty's life (on the orders of her strict mother). The relevant entries in the Diary were removed and destroyed by the future Mrs Kilvert. If the objections, as before, were Kilvert's lowly station in life they were soon to be removed (although the romance with Etty was not resurrected).

Kilvert was to meet the future Mrs Kilvert — Elizabeth Rowland — on a summer outing to Paris. She lived at Holly Bank, Wootton-by-Woodstock, near Blenheim Palace. Again the shy lady was to remove the details of their courtship from the Diary.

In April 1876 Kilvert is again called westwards and is offered

107

The Vicarage, Bredwardine

the living of St Harmon, near Rhayader, Powys. We know little of the year he spent at the lonely parish. The church was run-down and the parishioners scattered in an area where the non-conformist faith was strong. It has been suggested that the romance with Elizabeth was intensifying and Kilvert, thinking of a later marriage, decided St Harmon was too remote for the happiness of his future bride.

In 1877 he became vicar of Bredwardine where the splendid spacious vicarage overlooked his beloved River Wye — it was to be Kilvert's first and last home of his own. He was near enough to Clyro to meet his old friends again. Although some pages in the Diary are missing there are some interesting accounts of life around the parish. However, there are many words concerning Kilvert's failing health and psychic predictions of an early death.

Then, as suddenly as the Diaries began, the last entry was written for 13 March 1879. Kilvert was now contemplating marriage to Elizabeth Rowland and it may be that he had more than

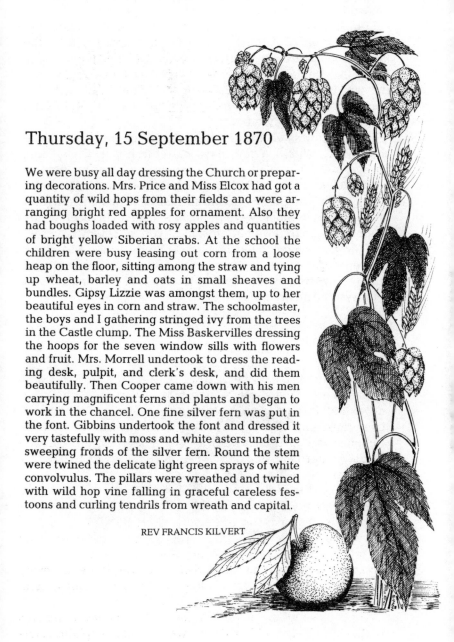

Thursday, 15 September 1870

We were busy all day dressing the Church or preparing decorations. Mrs. Price and Miss Elcox had got a quantity of wild hops from their fields and were arranging bright red apples for ornament. Also they had boughs loaded with rosy apples and quantities of bright yellow Siberian crabs. At the school the children were busy leasing out corn from a loose heap on the floor, sitting among the straw and tying up wheat, barley and oats in small sheaves and bundles. Gipsy Lizzie was amongst them, up to her beautiful eyes in corn and straw. The schoolmaster, the boys and I gathering stringed ivy from the trees in the Castle clump. The Miss Baskervilles dressing the hoops for the seven window sills with flowers and fruit. Mrs. Morrell undertook to dress the reading desk, pulpit, and clerk's desk, and did them beautifully. Then Cooper came down with his men carrying magnificent ferns and plants and began to work in the chancel. One fine silver fern was put in the font. Gibbins undertook the font and dressed it very tastefully with moss and white asters under the sweeping fronds of the silver fern. Round the stem were twined the delicate light green sprays of white convolvulus. The pillars were wreathed and twined with wild hop vine falling in graceful careless festoons and curling tendrils from wreath and capital.

REV FRANCIS KILVERT

enough now to occupy his time. Alternatively, Mrs Kilvert may have done further destructive work on the pages.

Francis Kilvert and Elizabeth were married at Wootton-by-Woodstock on 20 August 1879. They travelled north for the honeymoon, touring in the north-east of England and Scotland. When the couple returned to Bredwardine about a month later the wet weather did not dampen the enthusiastic welcome home. The village was decorated with flowers and bunting and many gifts were handed over.

The happiness of the Rev Kilvert and his bride was to be short-lived. Within a few days of returning to his village, Francis Kilvert was ill. On 23 September 1879 he died of peritonitis and was buried in the churchyard of his Bredwardine church. The Diaries, giving such an acute insight into rural life in Victorian times, were published in 1940; in recent years there has been renewed interest in Kilvert and many admirers of his writings come to pay homage at Bredwardine and Clyro. At Bredwardine there is a memorial seat where one can sit and admire the wooded hidden hills of the lovely borderland countryside and dream dreams . . .

Bredwardine Church Gate

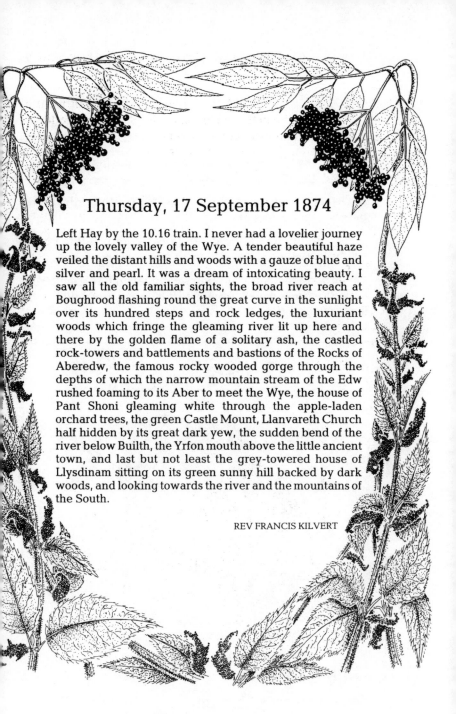

Thursday, 17 September 1874

Left Hay by the 10.16 train. I never had a lovelier journey up the lovely valley of the Wye. A tender beautiful haze veiled the distant hills and woods with a gauze of blue and silver and pearl. It was a dream of intoxicating beauty. I saw all the old familiar sights, the broad river reach at Boughrood flashing round the great curve in the sunlight over its hundred steps and rock ledges, the luxuriant woods which fringe the gleaming river lit up here and there by the golden flame of a solitary ash, the castled rock-towers and battlements and bastions of the Rocks of Aberedw, the famous rocky wooded gorge through the depths of which the narrow mountain stream of the Edw rushed foaming to its Aber to meet the Wye, the house of Pant Shoni gleaming white through the apple-laden orchard trees, the green Castle Mount, Llanvareth Church half hidden by its great dark yew, the sudden bend of the river below Builth, the Yrfon mouth above the little ancient town, and last but not least the grey-towered house of Llysdinam sitting on its green sunny hill backed by dark woods, and looking towards the river and the mountains of the South.

REV FRANCIS KILVERT

111

Rev Francis Kilvert Walk

1 Visit Kilvert's house (Ashbrook), church and churchyard *(the names on the graves appear in the Diaries)*.

2 At the junction take the lane signed Painscastle.

3 After 2 miles the main lane turns 90° to the left. Here keep straight ahead along a hedged track.

4 Back on the lane turn right. At a junction go through a metal gate to rough sheeplands.

5 Walk through another gate and bear slightly left to pass a solitary hawthorn tree and go alongside a wire fence.

6 Go through the corner railing gate. Stay in the same direction. By a broken wall turn 90° to the right. Drop down to the lane by a junction.

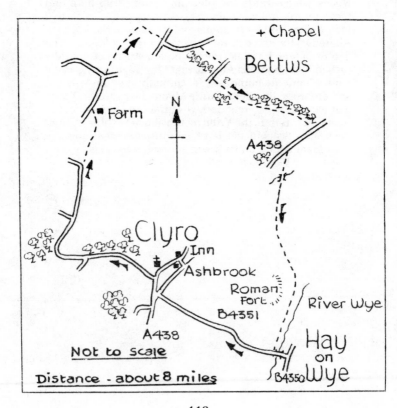

7 Take the lane signed Rhydspence. After ½ mile go through a gateway on the right.

8 Walk parallel to the right-hand wood and proceed through the fields to the lane. Turn right to Offa's Dyke signs.

9 Follow further signs to the A438. Turn right then pick up further Offa's Dyke signs.

10 The path crosses several fields to go between the Roman fort (on the right) and the River Wye (on the left).

11 At the B4351 turn right to Clyro village.

WTLL-H

When we think of Rudyard Kipling we immediately think of lands far overseas — the colonial Empire from India to South Africa — of 'The Road to Mandalay', *The Jungle Book* and the Elephant Boy.

Indeed, Kipling himself, perhaps the result of his early years, felt something of an alien in his own country.

He was born John Rudyard Kipling in Bombay on 30 December 1865. The first name was never used; the unusual second one was the result of a romantic meeting of his parents. Their first encounter was on Lake Rudyard, near Leek, in Staffordshire.

As was the habit of the upper classes of the Empire administrators, the children were placed in the hands of poorly paid servants — servants who were at the beck and call of their masters and mistresses. The little ones often became little terrors and Rudyard, by the time he returned to England with his mother when he was a little over two years old, was no exception. He was reported as being highly strung with a fiery temper.

The purpose of his mother's visit to England was to await the birth of her second child. The family (now increased by the addition of a daughter Alice, nicknamed Trix) went back to India. The children, thoroughly spoilt and cosseted by doting native servants, were soon to have their way of life shattered.

It was the common practice for Anglo-Indians to send their children to England to be educated in a more suitable climate. In answer to a newspaper advertisement, the Kiplings left Rudyard (then barely six) and Trix with formidable foster parents, Mr and Mrs Holloway, at a harsh-looking house called Lorne Lodge at Southsea.

Kipling later referred to this place as the 'House of Desolation', a 'Forlorn Lodge'. Excursions were few and certainly rarely to the countryside. He did visit an old gentleman away from the town — 'Here everything was wonderful and unlike my world,' he later wrote, '. . . and I played in hot, sweet smelling meadows and ate all sorts of things.'

Biographers have questioned the reasons for the Kiplings leaving their children in the care of strangers when there were

Lorne Lodge, Southsea

relations of standing (many with youngsters of similar ages to Rudyard and Trix). Perhaps the answer lies in recalling Rudyard's behaviour — his tantrums, his precociousness. The Holloways were paid to do a job — the fact that the life at Southsea was to young Rudyard an unexplained reversal of his previous supremacy may have made matters worse during the seven years at Lorne Lodge.

In *Baa, Baa Black Sheep*, a short story written in 1888, Kipling was to describe bitterly his experiences and severely castigated the Holloway family. Sister Trix had a different viewpoint: Mrs Holloway (Aunty Rose) had pined for a daughter and the pretty fair-haired little girl soon became her favourite, and the apotheosis was complete. Extravagant favours were accorded and she was to recall that Kipling's narrative was somewhat exaggerated.

A summer on a farm in Epping Forest followed. The children were initiated into the love of the rural ways, of which they were completely unaware. On the first morning of their stay the farmer, Mr Dally, informed them they could do what they liked — provided they did not leave gates open, throw stones at animals and break down orchard trees.

The Kiplings found a new school for Rudyard in 1878 at the United Services College, Westward Ho!, Devon. Discipline was severe, the buildings were unprepossessing, the food only tolerable and bullying common. However, things soon changed. Rudyard made good friends and was to indulge in mild escapades. He was considered a school intellectual.

For *Stalky and Co.* (published in 1899) he drew on characters and situations he knew at Westward Ho! His views, however, were probably clouded as the book was written some fifteen years after leaving the college.

Kipling left school when he was sixteen and a half. Back in India with his parents he worked on the *Civil and Military Gazette.* He started with conventional reporting, then switched to documentary pieces and occasional verses as end pieces. These poems were published in book form as *Departmental Ditties.* After he was promoted to the staff of a sister paper, *The Pioneer,* Kipling's first fiction work, *Plain Tales from the Hills,* was published in 1888. Although not successful in London, *Plain Tales* and subsequent editions, marketed by the Indian Railway Library, sold out in India.

Despite his success in India and his lack of literary fame back home, he was determined to return to England where 'there was something to do every night'. He travelled home by the east route via Burma, Singapore, Japan, America and Canada. He disliked the first two and loved the others. In October 1889, still not twenty-four, he arrived back in England.

Fame came fast, especially after his *Barrack Room Ballads* and stories had appeared in periodicals. The poems were often recited in music halls and smoking concerts.

In the following year he met Caroline Balestier, the sister of an American publisher, and married her. After their marriage the couple lived for four years on the Balestier estate, Vermont. The years were productive — Kipling's memory went back to his past experiences on the Indian sub-continent. The result was *The Jungle Book* and *The Second Jungle Book.*

After a dispute on the Vermont estate and tension between

The Glory of the Garden

Our England is a garden that is full of stately views,
Of borders, beds and shrubberies and lawns and avenues,
With statues on the terraces and peacocks strutting by;
But the Glory of the Garden lies in more than meets the eye.

For where the old thick laurels grow, along the thin red wall,
You will find the tool- and potting-sheds which are the heart of all;
The cold-frames and the hot-houses, the dungpits and the tanks,
The rollers, carts and drain-pipes, with the barrows and the planks.

And there you'll see the gardeners, the men and 'prentice boys
Told off to do as they are bid and do it without noise;
For, except when seeds are planted and we shout to scare the birds,
The Glory of the Garden is abideth not in words.

And some can pot begonias and some can bud a rose,
And some are hardly fit to trust with anything that grows;
But they can roll and trim the lawns and sift the sand and loam,
For the Glory of the Garden occupieth all who come.

Our England is a garden, and such gardens are not made
By singing:- 'Oh, how beautiful!' and sitting in the shade,
While better men than we go out and start their working lives
At grubbing weeds from gravel-paths with broken dinner-knives.

There's not a pair of legs so thin, there's not a head so thick,
There's not a hand so weak and white, nor yet a heart so sick,
But it can find some needful job that's crying to be done,
For the Glory of the Garden glorifieth every one.

Then seek your job with thankfulness and work till further orders
If it's only netting strawberries or killing slugs on borders;
And when your back stops aching and your hands begin to harden,
You will find yourself a partner in the Glory of the Garden.

Oh, Adam was a gardener, and God who made him sees
That half a proper gardener's work is done upon his knees,
So when your work is finished, you can wash your hands and pray
For the Glory of the Garden, that it may not pass away!
And the Glory of the Garden it shall never pass away!

RUDYARD KIPLING

The Way Through the Woods

They shut the road through the woods
Seventy years ago.
Weather and rain have undone it again,
And now you would never know
There was once a road through the woods
Before they planted the trees.
It is underneath the coppice and heath
And the thin anemones.
Only the keeper sees
That, where the ring-dove broods,
And the badgers roll at ease,
There was once a road through the woods.

Yet, if you enter the woods
Of a summer evening late,
When the night-air cools on the trout-ringed pools
Where the otter whistles his mate,
(They fear men not in the woods,
Because they see so few.)
You will hear the beat of a horse's feet,
And the swish of a skirt in the dew,
Steadily cantering through
The misty solitudes,
As though they perfectly knew
The old lost road through the woods . . .
But there is no road through the woods.

RUDYARD KIPLING

118

Bateman's

the USA and Britain, the Kiplings (now with two children) left for England. They settled in Sussex in the village of Rotting-dean.

Kipling came to the life of an English countryman as a complete outsider after his travels around the world. When he bought the Sussex country estate of Bateman's, Burwash, with its thirty-three acres of land, he grew to feel so much akin to the rural existence that this was to be his home until his death thirty-four years later.

This affinity was to be seen in two of his finest stories. Both *An Habitation Enforced* and *My Son's Wife* captured the outlook and sentiment of the old landed gentry. *Friendly Brook* sees the outlook of the other side — the labouring class and rustics on the estates. In *Puck of Pook's Hill* Kipling captured Sussex and wove the background subtly into the stories and legends that traced the history of our island.

'We discovered England, which we had never seen before, he wrote to his American friend, Charles Eliot Norton, in November 1902, 'and went to live in it. England is a wonderful land. It is the most marvellous of all foreign countries that I have ever been in. It is made up of trees and green fields and mud and the gentry and at last I'm one of the gentry.'

119

Rudyard Kipling Walk

1 From Burwash village take the lane by the war memorial.

2 At a junction turn right to Kipling's house, Bateman's.

3 Turn left along a farm drive over the River Dudwell.

4 Past the farm climb at the side of the meadow and wood.

5 Enter the woods through a hunting gate.

6 Cross the forest 'road'. Keep in the same general direction through the woods then bear right (edge of woodlands) to a lane.

7 Turn right to join the A265. Proceed right for 300 yards.

8 Turn left along a bridleway for 2 miles.

9 At the lane turn left then right at once (farm drive).

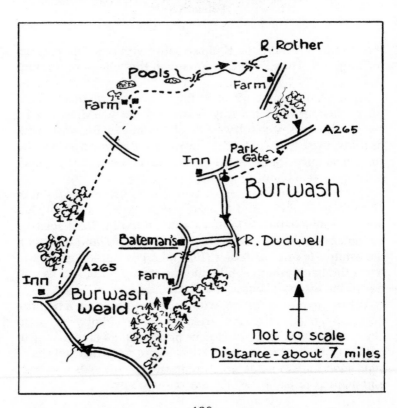

The doorway at Bateman's

10 Bear left at the junction to the farm. Veer right by the barns to rough pasture.

11 Keep to the right of the lakes to arable lands. At the brook turn left to a bridge over the river.

12 Follow the river downstream to the next bridge and go over the water. Bear right to the farm and lane.

13 Turn right for ¼ mile. Take the footpath on the left. Descend to the footbridge.

14 Climb over the brook (woods on the left) to the A265. Turn right.

15 Go through a kissing gate on the left by the park gates.

16 Walk alongside the drive and continue to Burwash church.

Information
Bateman's (National Trust) is open daily (except Fridays) from March to October.

North-east of Nottingham, the hilly countryside, no doubt once green and very beautiful, has been moulded by man's incessant search for the black gold, coal. So, today, spoil heaps disturb the contours of nature and row upon row of terraced houses were quickly erected, packed together like sardines where once there were woods and fields.

At the end of the last century the population of Eastwood, where D. H. Lawrence was born, was a little over 3,000. Within thirty years this number doubled and today it is nearer 12,000.

So the countryside of Lawrence has changed drastically since the days when he roamed in his childhood. However, it is still possible to walk along rural ways among the frequent reminders of the rich deposits of iron and coal that are below our feet.

Lawrence's father, Arthur, worked at the mines; he started at the Brinsley pit when he was seven years old. He met his wife Lydia at a Christmas party at his Aunt Alice's house. He was twenty-eight, she twenty-two, and a year later they were married and went to live in Victoria Street, Eastwood.

It was not a good match; Arthur Lawrence was a poor and uncultured miner; Lydia was the daughter of a Methodist lay preacher from a family that had once owned prosperous lace factories. She was a schoolteacher, well-versed with a love of literature; she wanted a life of piety. She attended the local chapel regularly and drink was an anathema to her. Arthur was the complete contrast and was especially a hard drinker. He worked on the 'butty' stall where miners were hired.

The income for the family was very limited and the situation was exacerbated by Arthur's expenditure on drink. The first child, George, arrived in 1876 then came Ernest in 1878 and Emily in 1882. To assist the family finances Mrs Lawrence sold linen and lace from the front room of her house. The house still stands and is now a museum.

On 11 September 1885, David Herbert Richard Lawrence was born. In 1887, with the arrival of a fifth child, Ada, the house at 8a Victoria Street was grossly overcrowded and the family moved to The Breach, Brinsley. The Breach was a rather elegant row of houses that backed on to a colliery. Arthur was hard-working in the house and although it was resented by his prim wife he loved recounting stories to the children and dancing and singing.

Bert, although a delicate child, went out on excursions into the woodlands and pastures. 'To me', he wrote, 'it seemed an extremely beautiful countryside.' Like his father he became interested in wild life. He attended Beauvale Board School and, no doubt encouraged by his articulate mother (who was determined to keep her sons out of the mines), was a good scholar. He did not like the rough play or games of the boys but preferred to be with the girls.

When he was six the family moved again; the better-class houses were on a higher land and this is where they went — to Walker Street. Bert was not to forget the view from the house, across to the woods and to Haggs Farm and the open countryside where he tramped with his sisters to pick the berries and leaves. He wrote a verse for his childhood friend:

> We sit in a lovely meadow,
> My sweetheart and me;
> And we are oh so happy
> Mid the flowers, birds and bees.

Victoria Street, Eastwood

The Breach, D. H. Lawrence's House

Sister Emily read stories to the younger children and this must have been appreciated by the embryo novelist in Bert.

Bert worked hard at his studies and was awarded a council scholarship to Nottingham High School. He made the long and arduous journey from the age of twelve and this affected the health of the boy who was never strong. Overall he was a good student and received a sound education until July 1901 when he left school.

Prompted by his brother Ernest, he applied for and obtained a post as a junior clerk at a Nottingham firm which manufactured surgical goods. Ernest caught pneumonia and died; three months after starting work Lawrence also suffered the same illness.

His mother, having lost one son, was now very protective; he attended the Congregational Chapel with the other children three times each Sunday. The British School adjoined the chapel and from 1902 until 1906 Lawrence taught general subjects and went for part-time teacher training at Ilkeston.

In 1905 the family moved again, this time to a house that overlooked open fields — 97 Lynn Croft. Lawrence was now observing people that he was to use later in his novels. Some characters were his fellow student teachers with whom he went on long walking excursions. Buildings too were to be recalled: Lamb Close House became Shortlands in *Women in Love* and Highclose in *The White Peacock*. Haggs Farm (where Jessie Chambers was an admiring teenager) was to be described in *Sons and Lovers.*

He was now an avid reader of anything he could lay his hands on, including the classics and the current popular novelists and poets. He began to write pieces himself with his poems stamping an individual style.

By diligent work he won an award to Nottingham University College and commenced his studies for an arts degree in 1906. The writing continued, sometimes secretly at home as his mother considered original writing (as opposed to studies) would interrupt his learning ability. It was at this time he began his first novel, *Laetitia,* which he completed in draft by the end of his first year at college.

He transferred to a non-degree course to give more time for his own writing and received his teaching certificate in June 1908. In the autumn he secured a teaching post at Croydon, and he left the close attention of his mother and his rural home ways around Haggs Farm and the sorrowful Jessie.

At first he disliked teaching, especially having to cope with the tough, indisciplined youngsters. His firm stance, however, and rather unorthodox approach paid off and he obtained the confidence of the pupils — and some good results. In his spare time at his lodgings he painted and continued with his literary output, again revising *Laetitia* (which was to be called *The White Peacock).*

Lawrence was referred to Ford Maddox Hueffer, editor of *The English Review* in 1909. After a meeting, Hueffer found a publisher for *The White Peacock* and also introduced him to many literary figures, such as W. B. Yeats and H. G. Wells. A selection of his poems appeared in *The English Review.*

Lawrence had a succession of girlfriends but found consolation and affection from his love from past days, Jessie Chambers. In the spring of 1909 he met Helen Corke, a friend of a fellow teacher at Croydon. She had had a torrid romantic affair with a married man on the Isle of Wight; the man hanged himself and Lawrence comforted the distraught Helen.

Helen had kept notes on the sad episode and Lawrence, on

Haggs Farm

reading the account, saw the plot of a novel. Within a few months the outline of *The Saga of Siegmund* was completed.

In 1910, when Lawrence's amorous involvements were particularly difficult, his mother became ill with cancer. With his emotional state confused, he met Louie Burrows, an old friend from his Eastwood and University days. As Mrs Lawrence was dying, an advance copy of the published *The White Peacock* was received. She was too ill to read it.

Lawrence proposed to Louie, then had second thoughts and returned to Helen Corke, but his proposal to her was rejected. Later, in 1911, he again developed pneumonia and wrote to Louie that the doctor had advised him against marriage. She never saw him again. He resigned his post at Croydon and felt isolated — that all was now lost.

However, *The White Peacock* had been well received and there were offers to publish *The Saga of Siegmund,* now called *The Trespasser.* Poems also appeared regularly but Lawrence was not able to exist solely on his literary output.

He thought about teaching in Germany and sought advice from his former teacher of French at Nottingham College, Professor Weekley. He met Mrs Freida Weekley, the teacher's wife and they fell in love; in May 1912 they went off to live together in Germany.

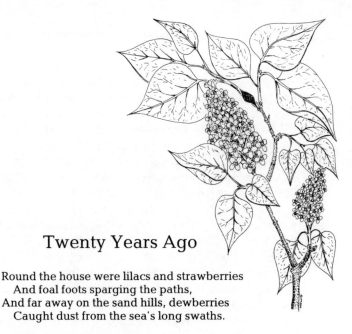

Twenty Years Ago

Round the house were lilacs and strawberries
   And foal foots sparging the paths,
And far away on the sand hills, dewberries
   Caught dust from the sea's long swaths.

Up the wolds the woods were walking
   And nuts fell out of their hair
At the gate the nets hung, balking
   The star-lit rush of a hare.

In the autumn fields, the stubble
   Tinkled the music of gleaning.
At a mother's knee, the trouble
   Lost all its meaning.

Yea, what good beginnings
   To this sad end!
Have we had our innings?
   God forfend!

D. H. LAWRENCE

For several years Lawrence had worked on *Sons and Lovers* — again set in the region of his youth. It was completed in 1912 (while Lawrence and Freida were staying on Lake Garda, Italy) and published with *Love Poems* the following year. In June Lawrence and Freida returned to England; Freida's divorce was finalised and she became Mrs Lawrence in July.

Lawrence's literary output continued, still frequently using incidents recalled from the past. Often passages from the books were thought distasteful; Lawrence was taken to court over *The Rainbow* and the magistrates declared the book obscene and ordered all copies to be destroyed.

Utterly disillusioned the Lawrences moved to Cornwall. It was the time of the First World War and there was hostile reaction from the locals, especially because of Freida's German ancestry and Lawrence's anti-war stance. In 1917 the Lawrences were officially ordered to leave the county.

They settled in London, then Derbyshire. *Women in Love* was brought out in 1920 in America (where a court action to stop it failed) and in 1921 in Britain. *Aaron's Rod* was published the following year.

After the Armistice there was much travelling — Capri, Sicily, Ceylon, Australia (where *Kangaroo* was set), New Mexico and New York. New Mexico captivated the Lawrences and they envisaged a Utopian colony in the mountains.

Returning to Italy in 1925 after an attack of tuberculosis, the zeal for writing returned and Lawrence started on his last masterpiece, *Lady Chatterley's Lover.* The plan was that it would be privately printed and distributed; Lawrence knew that his candid and honest view of love would not be acceptable to the general public. In the book he again remembered the landscapes of the Midlands, its scenes, its houses and people.

The book was completed in 1923 and surreptitiously distributed world-wide to subscribers. The reception in England was as anticipated. 'A shameful book', one critic said. Lawrence was also publically castigated by officials for some of his erotic paintings and a book of poems.

In 1929 he became gravely ill and on 2 March 1930 he died at Vence, southern France. His cremated remains were taken in 1935 to a place far distant from his homeland — to the mountain retreat in New Mexico. Sadly it was only many years after his death that D. H. Lawrence was recognised as the writer of some of the finest novels in the English language.

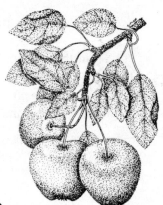

Letter from Town:
on a Grey Morning in March

The clouds are pushing in grey reluctance slowly northward to you,
　While north of them all, at the farthest ends, stands one bright-
　　　　　　　　　　　　　　　　　　bosomed, a glance
With fire as it guards the wild north coasts, red-fire seas running through
　The rocks where ravens flying to windward melt as a well-shot lance.
You should be out by the orchard, where violets secretly darken the
　　　　　　　　　　　　　　　　　　earth,
　Or there in the woods of the twilight, with northern wind-flowers
　　　　　　　　　　　　　　　　　　shaken astir.
Think of me here in the library, trying and trying a song that is worth
　Tears and swords to my heart, arrows no armour will turn or deter.
You tell me the lambs have come, they lie like daisies white in the grass
　Of the dark-green hills; new calves in shed; peewits turn after the
　　　　　　　　　　　　　　　　　　plough —
It is well for you. For me the navvies work in the road where I pass
　And I want to smite in anger the barren rock of each waterless brow.
Like the sough of a wind that is caught up high in the mesh of budding
　　　　　　　　　　　　　　　　　　trees,
　A sudden car goes sweeping past, and I strain my ear to hear
The voice of the furtive triumphant engine as it rushes past like a breeze,
　To hear on its mocking triumphance unwitting the after-echo of fear.

D. H. LAWRENCE

129

D. H. Lawrence Walk

1 From the car park by the Craft Centre turn into Victoria Street *(birthplace)*.

2 Continue to Nottingham Road and turn left to pass the site of the Congregational Church.

3 Opposite the War Memorial take a left turn into Walker Street. *The Lawrence family moved to No 8 in 1892 and this was their home until 1905. Their next house was in nearby Lynn Croft.*

4 Just after the school turn left down a tarmac path to Orchard Road.

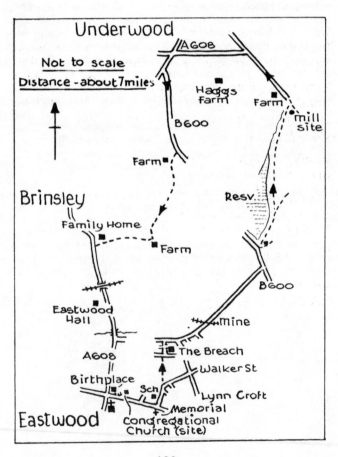

5 Here at No 26 *(it was No 57 The Breach)* is where Lawrence lived from 1887 to 1892. Go down the road to the left of the house.

6 Go over the crossroads to Greenhills Road and turn right.

7 Keep ahead at the junctions and go through a mine complex to join the B600 at Moorgreen.

8 Turn left for ¼ mile then right at a bridleway by the reservoir. Stay on the track near the reservoir and feeder stream. *There are fine bluebell woods here at springtime.*

9 By the mill site join the farm track and turn left when the track becomes a lane. At the junction turn left (signed Underwood). Through a gateway 200 yards before the main road we can see Haggs Farm.

10 On the A608 at Underwood turn left then left again along the B600. After ½ mile turn right through a white gate and go along the farm drive. Keep on the track to a second farm.

11 Turn right (there is a wall on the left). The path is signed Brinsley at the corner of the wood. Go through the gate and walk on the left-hand boundary of the field and around an old hut.

12 Climb the track to the road. *Lawrence's grandparents lived in the house on the right.*

13 Turn left on the A608. The road goes by the walls of the grounds to Eastwood Hall *(home of mine owners, the Walker family, now National Coal Board headquarters).*

14 The road leads to Eastwood.

Information
Birthplace Museum is open daily.

Why are the Beatrix Potter books so very popular with children — and at least one adult — eighty years or so after they were written? Perhaps the answer is that they were not just well written but exquisitely drawn and so delicately coloured with a fine detailed perception of nature. This observation was the result of Beatrix Potter's great affection, in her lonely childhood and middle-life, of her pets such as the rabbit called Peter, mice like Tom Thumb and Hunca Munca, and the hedgehog, Mrs Tiggy-Winkle.

There was also enchantment of the countryside of the lowland Lake District where she spent long holidays and was, in later years, to live permanently. For the backcloths to the illustrations of many of the simple stories, Beatrix took the views of northern landscapes and gardens she knew and loved.

Beatrix Potter (christened Helen Beatrix) was born on 28 July 1866. She was the first child of Mr and Mrs Rupert Potter who lived in very comfortable surroundings at No 2, Bolton Gardens, Kensington. (The house was destroyed in the London bombings of 1940.) It was, in those days, a good upper-class area; the house had a good complement of servants when service jobs were avidly sought. Beatrix was put into the charge of a rather stern Scottish nurse, McKenzie.

Although not unhappy, she was conditioned to a rather lonely and isolated existence. Holidays were invariably spent in a furnished house in Scotland; the servants would be transferred to carry on with the usual rituals of the household, including the morning walk for Beatrix, led by McKenzie.

The family's wealthy status was the result of fortunes made by earlier generations in the Lancashire cotton industry. The Potters could therefore enjoy their life without having to think about doing any real work. Beatrix's father had trained as a barrister but never had recourse to use the knowledge gained, and he spent much of his 'working' day at his favourite London clubs and enjoying his new-fangled hobby of photography.

Beatrix was brought up as a Unitarian although the family were not strict in their religious observance. When she was five, a brother, Bertram, arrived in the household. Beatrix was taught privately at home but loved to listen to, and glean information from, an intellectual and interesting grandmother, Mrs Edmund Potter, who had many tales to tell. Beatrix would often sit taking copious and secret notes of the old lady's stories of her exciting upbringing in Lancashire, as one of nine sisters. (One recalls that the Brontës also wrote minute records.) Beatrix started her secret journal of coded mysterious jottings which she maintained until she was over thirty — it was discovered, in 1952, in her cottage at Sawrey and for many years the code could not be deciphered.

In her loneliness, she subconsciously adopted many of the traits of her grandmother — the forthright manner and determination — that were to stand her in good stead in future years.

The isolation of Beatrix was complete again when Bertram went away to Charterhouse School. She was kept at home, meeting no schoolchildren or playmates and it was not surprising, when added to the inattention of her parents, that she became, while still basically happy, a very shy child with the correlated problem of difficulty in expressing herself.

She was taught during the formative years by the governess, Miss Hammond. Miss Hammond was a gentle and kind lady, well liked by Beatrix. Her interest in nature study and art was transmitted to her pupil. Beatrix was also given more formal art lessons for some years by a Miss Cameron. When Miss Hammond thought she had conveyed all she knew to Beatrix, the young teenage girl was left to her own devices. (Later Beatrix was to infer that this isolation created an originality so indispensible to an author.) Other governesses were to follow until she was about eighteen.

The Scottish vacations were less isolated; in the holiday house with her brother she could explore the beautiful world of nature that had been described by Miss Hammond. She was both inquisitive and fascinated by what she saw and felt an immediate affinity with country life and the folk associated with it. She would tour farms and cottages and make friends with the animals, both domestic and wild. Plants, animals and flowers were carefully sketched; all the folios carefully gathered together to form a book. Some flowers were pressed and drawn later at Bolton Gardens.

With a foretaste of what was to come, Beatrix occasionally showed an item of clothing on her animals. On later holidays, she took her animal friends with her; Peter, the rabbit, in a hutch and Tiggy, the hedgehog, in a basket. On the return journey the rabbit would be carried under an arm with the hutch full of assorted bric-a-brac — the natural history specimens and odd items of clothing. Holidays were now spread between the seaside, Scotland and the Lake District.

There was no question of a career for Beatrix; in her wealthy surroundings there was just not the need of gainful employment for a daughter. She decided she would be an artist; she would tour the Natural History Museum and art galleries near her home; she would examine specimens under the microscope and draw plants, animals and flowers in meticulous detail. She became especially interested in fungi and she thought about a book on the subject, including her drawings and paintings. However, her enthusiasm was dashed by staid and authoritarian academics.

From the serious work, to relieve the boredom of inactivity, she retreated into the world of her rabbits and mice; to amuse her cousins she made drawings of families of these little animals in their semi-human world. She illustrated her letters with animal drawings and amused little children with her stories and instant pictures. Many letters containing stories and fine drawings of her rabbit went to young Noel Moore, the sick son of one of Beatrix's governesses.

A friend of the family, Canon Rawnsley, encouraged Beatrix in her artistic talents; they had a common interest in the study and love of nature. The Canon was a formidable figure; he was a dedicated champion for the protection of the Lake District against the attack from trippers and the railway companies who would convey them in their masses to desecrate the lonely beauty. (His ardent campaigning for the countryside resulted in the formation of the National Trust in 1895.)

There were endless discussions between Canon Rawnsley and Beatrix Potter. The encouragement and friendship of the clergyman resulted in the completion of Beatrix's first complete work, *The Tale of Peter Rabbit.*

Beatrix had thought that the tales in the letters which were so enthusiastically received by children would make a little book. She retrieved the letters from Noel Moore and sent the manuscript and drawings to Frederick. Warne and Company, the publishers suggested by Canon Rawnsley. The rejection note was the first of many; Beatrix was not discouraged, showing that determination that was so characteristic of her grandmother. She decided to publish and sell the book herself.

She had two hundred and fifty of the little books printed in black and white and found a ready market among her friends and relations, selling them at a price of one shilling and twopence. With the second print complete, Beatrix again contracted Warnes. They now accepted the work, provided the illustrations were coloured.

She soon started on another work, *The Tailor of Gloucester,* which was based on an illustrated letter story to Noel's sister Freda. She did not think Warnes would want another book so soon so Beatrix again paid for a private edition, limited to five hundred copies. This was to be her 'mouse book'.

Next, Beatrix chose a 'squirrel book' and *The Tale of Squirrel Nutkin* appeared from Warnes in 1903 and immediately became a best seller. Although she was well over thirty, Beatrix's parents began to be dissatisfied about the time she was spending writing and negotiating with publishers. Mr and Mrs Potter did not like her to be less dependent on them and correctly suspected that there might have been a romance between their daughter and Norman Warne, the son of the old publisher Frederick Warne. In the class-conscious era of the early

Beatrix Potter's Hill Top Farm

135

twentieth century, to think of marrying a tradesman — a publisher — was unacceptable.

More books, *The Tale of Benjamin Bunny* and *The Tale of Two Bad Mice,* followed with inspiration coming on the long holidays in the Lake District. She made sketches of Cumbrian landscapes to use later.

Each stage of the books was discussed with Norman Warne. The friendship blossomed to a proposal in 1905 which Beatrix, now almost forty, accepted in spite of her parents' disfavour.

Their happiness was to be short-lived. Within a few months Norman suddenly became ill and died.

Beatrix that summer had further shown her independence and purchased Hill Top Farm at Sawrey in the Lake District that she so loved. She knew the children here and had given them copies of her books. She knew the simple farming folk and, a northerner by descent, felt at home in the countryside. She left the former tenant farmer in charge and, with alterations completed, spent all the time she could at the house.

The preparation of further books continued and sketches were made of the inside of the rooms at Hill Top for backgrounds. Thirteen books came in the next eight years, many based on Sawrey and the farm. *Jemima Puddle-Duck,* in particular, shows farmyard views very little different from those of today, eighty years later, and *The Roly-Poly Pudding,* the outside of Hill Top. *The Pie and the Patty Pan* has a dedication 'to the children of Sawrey'.

In 1909, Beatrix Potter increased her landholding by the purchase of Castle Farm, not far from Hill Top. She was advised by William Heelis, a solicitor who handled the purchase. Beatrix was suffering from depression, following a bout of illness, which was brought on perhaps because of an offer of marriage from Mr Heelis which had to be discussed with her family. The reaction of her parents was the opposition she had anticipated — even though she was now forty-seven years old.

With the large royalty payments still being received, Beatrix looked for more property to buy. In the summer of 1913, she and William Heelis became engaged in secret; they were married at Kensington Parish Church in October and set up home at Sawrey.

The change was not just a change of name. From now on she had cast off her old isolated spinster image; her creative writing was largely finished; now she was an outward-looking con-

Castle Farm

tented solicitor's wife and part-time farmer. She wrote little more although she was persuaded, as late as 1927, by an American publisher, to create *The Fairy Caravan*. However, it does not bear comparison with her earlier work. Her retreat from fame was complete. Beatrix shunned interviews, eagerly adopted her married name and even created the impression among her admirers that she had passed away.

In her own rural community, Beatrix was again isolated from the outside world but this time from choice and, with great happiness, content to be with her husband, living a simple life. The contrast with the London scene of strict social codes and behaviour was absolute.

Still Beatrix and William acquired property. In 1923, it was Troutbeck Park — a lonely farm estate covering over two thousand acres of fell land. Most of it was given over to sheep of the Herdwick breed and Beatrix became a dedicated, hard-working and respected farmer. Other farms were purchased with the aims of the National Trust in mind as a future guardian of large tracts of her beloved Lake District. Besides giving financial aid to the Trust, she was also a tireless worker.

Beatrix Potter prized the rewards of old age, especially the loving and happy relationship with William. With health failing towards the end of the 1930s she made her will, remembering the National Trust and her employees. The winter of 1943 brought the end — a chill which developed into bronchitis. She died on 22 December 1943, aged seventy-seven, gazing over her winter-clothed Lakeland hills.

THE TALE OF SQUIRREL NUTKIN

by **BEATRIX POTTER**

F. WARNE & Cº LTD

THIS is a Tale about a tail— a tail that belonged to a little red squirrel, and his name was Nutkin.

He had a brother called Twinkleberry, and a great many cousins: they lived in a wood at the edge of a lake.

9

THE TALE OF PETER RABBIT

by

BEATRIX POTTER

F. WARNE & Cᵒ LTᴰ

ONCE upon a time there were four little Rabbits, and their names were—

Flopsy,
Mopsy,
Cotton-tail,
and Peter.

They lived with their Mother in a sand-bank, underneath the root of a very big fir-tree.

9

Beatrix Potter Walk

1 After visiting Hill Top (car park nearby), turn right along the B5285 towards Hawkshead. Turn right through a kissing gate (signed St Peter's Church).

2 Cross a brook. Bear left to a lane to the left of a white farm. Visit St Peter's Church, *(fine stained glass in St Cecilia window and notes from Beethoven's 5th symphony).*

3 On the lane again turn right. At a T-junction cross to a signed bridleway. After ½ mile bear left (path signed Hawkshead — HH).

4 Climb to the junction of bridleways and take the track signed Claife Heights. Stay on the main track to border a tarn. At the division take the left-hand track.

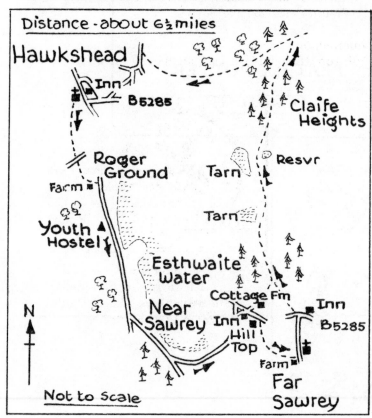

5 Through a gate in the wall the track is above the tarn and to the left of the reservoir. The path leads to some woods. Stay on the main track. Keep on the forest 'road' signed HH.

6 *Take care!* Almost at the top of a rise turn left off the road (there is a clear sign HH). Through a gate the path gradually drops downhill to a lane.

7 Turn left then right at a junction to the pretty Hawkshead village. Go through a gate at the far corner in the church-yard. In the meadow walk by a stone wall.

8 Through a kissing gate turn left (signed Roger Ground). At the lane turn right for 100 yards and then left by a pillar box. At the end of the lane go through a little white gate to a field.

9 Walk by the left-hand side of the field. Skirt the farm to join the drive and the lane. Turn right. Follow the lane past the Youth Hostel to Near Sawrey.

Information
Hill Top (National Trust) is open daily from April to October.

Below the peaks of the Eildon Hills the River Tweed twists a meandering way in a wide vale.

Melrose is sited here with its splendid ruined Cistercian abbey. It was to the border moorlands that Walter Scott came as a child. He fell in love with the area and was to come back in later years to build his magnificent mansion of Abbotsford, some four miles from Melrose. (The abbey was to feature in several of Scott's narrative poems and novels.)

He chose the site carefully so that he could view the fine panoramic scenery — the distant Cheviots, the Moorfoot Hills and the wooded Eildons, and in front Ettrick Water and the Ettrick Forest. It was to this region that Scott was to return both to live and to find the stimulation and atmosphere for his work.

Sir Walter Scott's father was also Walter Scott, who trained as a lawyer and was appointed to the privileged position of Writer to the Signet. He was a precise and conscientious man, both in his work and his religious life. (He was a strict Presbyterian and this was recalled by his son with some displeasure by 'the discipline of the Presbyterian Sabbath'. Scott's mother, Anne, was the daughter of a Professor of Medicine at Edinburgh University. She was privately educated in Edinburgh, followed by a finishing school.

After their marriage, the Scotts lived in Old Town, Edinburgh, at College Wynd or Close. The city at that time was dirty, smoky and unhealthy. Of the first six children born to Anne Scott, none lived beyond infancy. However, at the time of Walter's birth on 15 August 1771, there were grandiose plans to expand Edinburgh with well-planned streets. The Scotts moved to the newly laid-out elegant George Square when Walter was only a few months old. Although the air was now cleaner and the surroundings more healthy, the youngster developed polio and for the rest of his life was crippled.

The medical grandfather suggested that country air and rural walks would aid recovery. He was sent to a farm owned by his other grandfather at Sandy Knowe in the valley of the Tweed and the young Walter Scott fell in love with the Scottish countryside. 'It is here', wrote Scott '. . . that I have the first consciousness of existence.' Indeed, Abbotsford, where Scott was

Sir Walter Scott's Birthplace, Edinburgh, from an old print

to build his vast, castellated home, was only ten miles away.

On these country excursions into the borderlands he heard of the history of the Jacobites and the Battle of Culloden. He absorbed the folklore and stories of heroism, glory and patriotism and began to use his imagination to sow the seeds for future novels.

When he was four, Walter journeyed to Bath with an aunt, as it was thought his lameness could be helped by the thermal waters. On the way he visited historical sites in London, such as the Tower of London. He was to stay a year in Bath, to be followed by spells at the seaside and at Sandy Knowe. It was then felt that all that could be done for the affected leg had been done and Walter returned to stay at George Square, where there were now four brothers and a sister.

He was encouraged by his mother to read poetry and, in 1779, was sent to Edinburgh High School when he was eight years old. Although he was studying Latin, the language in isolation was not what interested Scott, but the door it opened to the store of knowledge of ancient history. He learnt to read the great national narrative poems in the original languages. In addition, Walter had a private home tutor. Throughout his schooldays he was an avid reader, with especial emphasis on travel books and history and the ballads and songs of folk culture.

In 1783, he left the High School and spent some months with an aunt in Kelso. It is interesting to note Scott's observation on his stay. He said he remembered

> distinctly the awaking of that delightful feeling for the beauties of natural objects which has never since deserted me. The neighbourhood of Kelso, the most beautiful, if not the most romantic village in Scotland, is eminently calculated to awaken these ideas. It presents objects, not only grand in themselves, but venerable from their association.

In November 1783, Walter entered Edinburgh University. He was still only twelve but this early age was not unusual in Scotland. He studied humanity (Latin), then later logic and metaphysics. His studies were suspended in 1786 when he suffered a severe haemorrhage and was very ill.

Not being allowed to talk, Walter read profusely, especially romantic novels and military history. With his recovery at Kelso he began to study law. This was followed by the start of his five-year apprenticeship with his father.

On his training he made trips into the borderlands, the Highlands and the countryside of Rob Roy. He explored the sites of the old battles and their history and stored in his retentive memory the anecdotes and detail that were to prove so useful.

Early in the summer of 1792 he was called to the Bar and then went off touring the border countryside, and journeyed into England. He visited Northumberland to see the Roman sites, but the trip was cut short when bad weather was encountered in the Lake District.

In the autumn, Scott went on what he called 'raids' to the 'wild and inaccessible' land of Liddesdale. He picked up material on ballads that he would later incorporate in *The Minstrelsy of the Scottish Border.* With a friend he spent much time in the Perthshire Highlands and heard of anecdotes of Rob Roy. Further excursions were made to the Trossachs and Loch Katrine — experiences that would be recalled in *The Lady of the Lake.*

He became interested in the German literary world and in 1796 his first published work was a translation. It was issued anonymously but a translation under his own name of a Goethe play was published in 1799.

After a broken love affair he met Charlotte Carpentier, a French girl of twenty-seven, on a visit to the English Lake District in 1797. It was a hasty romance and on Christmas Eve, Charlotte and Walter Scott were married.

In the same year, with Britain's current disputes with France, there was fear of an invasion. Scott joined the newly formed Edinburgh Volunteer Light Dragoons.

He settled with his bride in Edinburgh but also had a cottage in the village of Lasswade beside the River Esk, some six miles from the city.

In 1799 Scott was made Sheriff of Selkirkshire — the salary was £300. The work was not onerous and gave Scott time to work on ballads. In the same year the Scotts' first child, Sophia, was born.

The first two volumes of ballads were published in 1802 and were well received; another volume came the next year. In 1805 a long narrative poem *The Lay of the Last Minstrel* was so acclaimed and successful that Scott made the decision to be first and foremost a writer.

Scott received income and property from his late uncle's estate. He gave up the Eskdale cottage because it was not in the county of Selkirkshire, as his legal position demanded.

There were three more children: Walter born in 1801, Anne a couple of years later and the youngest was Charles, born in 1805.

A small house was rented at Ashestiel in the summer of 1804.

Abbotsford

It was on the southern bank of the Tweed and this was to be the Scotts' country retreat for eight years.

The Lay of the Last Minstrel was printed by Ballantynes, which was owned by an old school friend, James Ballantyne. A stake in the work was purchased by the Edinburgh publisher Archibald Constable. The success of the book put financial pressures on Ballantyne's printing business. Scott had resources, including the legacy from his uncle, and he lent cash to his friend. He now had a say in running the firm and, with grandiose ideas in association with other publishers, obtained large printing orders.

He had various legal and political posts but continued with his literary work and the narrative poem *Marmion* (1808) was followed by *The Lady of the Lake* (1810). This was probably the finest of his poems. At much the same time Scott worked on his edition of Dryden — this also appeared in 1808.

In 1809, after a rift with Constable, he founded John Ballantyne and Company (publishers) in opposition. This firm published *The Lady of the Lake,* which was an immediate success with many successive editions issued. Tourists thronged to Loch Katrine and the Trossachs, and the way to the Highlands for the masses was open. Scott presented Scotland as a place of great beauty with a peaceful present but a historic, interesting and often bloody past.

When the lease at Ashestiel ran out in 1811, Walter Scott bought a small farm by the Tweed, near Melrose. At once he talked of additions and expensive plans and the vast towered

Hunting Song

Waken, lords and ladies gay,
On the mountain dawns the day,
All the jolly chase is here,
With hawk, and horse, and hunting spear!
Hounds are in their couples yelling,
Hawks are whistling, horns are knelling,
Merrily, merrily, mingle they,
'Waken, lords and ladies gay.'

Waken, lords and ladies gay,
The mist has left the mountain grey,
Springlets in the dawn are steaming,
Diamonds on the brake are gleaming;
And foresters have busy been,
To track the buck in thicket green;
Now we come to chant our lay,
'Waken, lords and ladies gay.'

Waken, lords and ladies gay,
To the greenwood haste away;
We can show you where he lies,
Fleet of foot, and tall of size;
We can show the marks he made,
When 'gainst the oak his antlers fray'd;
You shall see him brought to bay,
'Waken, lords and ladies gay.'

Louder, louder chant the lay,
Waken, lords and ladies gay!
Tell them youth, and mirth and glee,
Run a course as well as we;
Time, stern huntsman! who can baulk,
Stanch as hound, and fleet as hawk:
Think of this, and rise with day,
Gentle lords and ladies gay.

SIR WALTER SCOTT

147

mansion of Abbotsford took shape over the next twelve years. Estates adjoining were secured.

While writing early in the day and carrying on with his legal work, Scott entertained lavishly many eminent nobility and men of letters.

With Byron more to the public taste in the next years Scott turned to prose, in fact to a work he had commenced in 1805 but put away, *Waverley*. With the rift now healed, Constable published it anonymously in 1814. The following year came *Guy Mannering* and *The Land of the Isles* (a narrative poem).

However, in spite of the popularity of the *Waverley* novels, Scott's vast spending on Abbotsford took its toll. He was almost bankrupt in 1813. The firm of John Ballantyne and Company was wound up but the printers, James Ballantyne and Company, continued. With the precarious financial situation Scott went on to produce, on average, a novel a year. In 1818 he was made a baronet.

After nine novels (the latter ones written while suffering from gall stones) based on Scotland and her history in 1820, Scott turned to medieval England with *Ivanhoe*. Fourteen books came in six years, including *Kenilworth,* set in the age of the first Elizabeth.

Scott paid off his personal debts, but business interests tied up with Constables and Ballantynes were based on paper credit. When his son (also Walter) married in 1825, Scott settled the Abbotsford estate on him to be realised after his death. This was subject to the possibility of raising £10,000 on mortgage against the estate if found necessary. In December the situation was desperate and the £10,000 was borrowed — to no avail. Early in the New Year Scott was a ruined man. Within months his wife and helpmate, Charlotte, passed away.

Scott continued to live at Abbotsford (now owned by his son) and wrote further novels, and still showed splendid hospitality.

With recurring ill health, Scott went on a cruise to the Mediterranean in 1831. He returned to his beloved Abbotsford in Tweedsdale the following July and died on 21 September.

The Violet

The violet in her greenwood bower,
   Where birchen boughs with hazels mingle,
May boast itself the fairest flower
   In glen, or copse, or forest dingle.

Though fair her gems of azure hue,
   Beneath the dewdrop's weight reclining;
I've seen an eye of lovelier blue,
   More sweet through wat'ry lustre shining.

The summer sun that dew shall dry,
   Ere yet the day be past its morrow;
Nor longer in my false love's eye
   Remain'd the tear of parting sorrow.

SIR WALTER SCOTT

Sir Walter Scott Walk

1 From the Market Square, Melrose, walk along the B6359 southwards. After ¼ mile go down the steps on the left (Eildon Walk signpost). The path soon climbs.

2 Go over a stile into a meadow. Continue climbing. Ignore the next stile on the right. At the corner cross a farm track. Keep at the side of the next field. Climb the stile to rough moorland and turn left.

3 Ignore minor paths and sheep runs but stay on the clear path. After ¾ mile turn left at the beech and pine woods to join the A6091. Turn right then left down a wide track.

4 Under an old railway bridge turn left to the B6361. Turn left (Dean Road) then immediately right through a kissing gate. A good path leads to estate roads. Stay on the lower road then go ahead along a tarmac fenced pathway to the Abbey and the road. *Note Scott's coachman's grave.*

5 Turn right past the Abbey and the Motor Museum. After ¼ mile the road bears sharp right. Turn left down a lane to a suspension bridge *(built 1826)*. Keep ahead along a footpath by the River Tweed.

6 Soon climb the steps and turn right to border the church green. Walk by a wall to a lane. Turn right to go through a kissing gate back to the river.

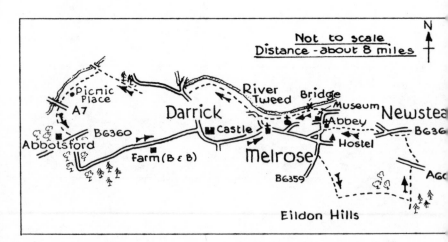

7 Just before a high road bridge go through a gate and over the stiles to the B6360. Cross to the lane.

8 After ⅓ mile (by the woods on the left) turn left to an old railway track. Turn right to the bridge. Turn left to a riverside path to a picnic place.

9 Follow the cinder path to the A7. Cross over to a woodland path to the B6360 and Abbotsford.

10 Take the lane by a phone box that leads past Darrick Castle *(which Scott tried to buy before building Abbotsford)* to Melrose.

Information
Abbotsford is open daily from mid March to the end of October.

WILLIAM SHAKESPEARE

I know a bank whereon the wild thyme blows,
Where oxlips and the nodding violet grows,
Quite over-canopied with luscious woodbine,
With sweet musk-roses, and with eglantine.

A Midsummer Night's Dream

There is a tiny timbered building in the back of a garden at Snitterfield — a little hamlet half a dozen miles from Stratford-upon-Avon. Here, the villagers would have us believe, a tenant farmer, Richard Shakespeare, lived in the fifteenth century. The lands were owned by the Ardens, a family who prospered in spite of being of Anglo-Saxon stock in a country conquered by the Normans. By the beginning of the sixteenth century, Robert Arden was Lord of the Manor beyond the woodlands at Wilmcote.

Richard Shakespeare had two sons, Henry and John, who were christened in the hilltop church adjacent to the cottage at Snitterfield. When of age, Henry assisted his father on the farm. His brother John was ambitious and eager to leave the rural by-ways for the town, and in about 1550 he became apprentice glovemaker in Stratford.

It was an age of elegant dressing by the nobility and the glove trade was buoyant. John, having made some money, remembered Mary Arden, the daughter of the Lord of the Manor. Robert Arden died in 1556 and John, as ever with an eye on business, married his Mary. (There was no church at Wilmcote and the ceremony is thought to have taken place in the church at nearby Aston Cantlow.)

John and Mary Shakespeare were now affluent with John's thriving glovemaking business and Mary's farm at Wilmcote, together with the share of her father's vast estate.

John became an alderman and they settled in a modest home in Henley Street. It was there that William (their third child) was born in the April of 1564.

The precise birthday is uncertain and we now place it (appropriately for the greatest of Englishmen) on St George's Day — 23 April.

Mary Arden's House, Wilmcote

Little is known about the childhood of the young Will — most of the life attributed to him is supposition. There were the learned activities of the Guild in the town and next door the Grammar School. The Shakespeares could certainly have afforded to send William here for a sound classical education.

The countryside around the town was readily accessible and, without doubt, the energetic lad roamed the remnants of the ancient Forest of Arden to the north. His knowledge of the ever-changing pattern of nature would have been gleaned and the local folk of Hampton-in-Arden insist today that *As You Like It* is set thereabouts.

But Will met the rustics too and quickly became involved in their world of poaching, wenching and drinking. The tale is told of the deer-stealing escapades in the elegant parklands of Charlecote, the home of Sir Thomas Lucy.

Although the Victorians liked to think of the Bard as the apex of moral living (there was a *Family Shakespeare* which expurgated all the unsavoury, if colourful, references), there is little doubt that he was a lover both of tavern life and of the fair sex at a very early age.

The saying in the Midland shires tells that Shakespeare went on drinking contests with:

Piping Pebworth, Dancing Marston,
Haunted Hillborough, Hungry Grafton,
Dodging Exhall; Papist Wixford,
Beggarly Broom and Drunken Bidford.

One of his wenching expeditions was to Shottery — now a western suburb of Stratford but in the seventeenth century a hamlet reached along rural lanes. Here lived Richard Hathaway and his many children. The eldest was Anne, and at twenty-six considered a little too old for wedlock.

William was eighteen and by November 1582, Anne was bearing his child. Shakespeare applied to the Bishop of Worcester for a special licence that would allow him to marry with only one reading of the banns. The licence reads 'Willelmum Shaxpere and Annam Whateley de Temple Grafton'. (Temple Grafton is a village some five miles distant — how the clerk made an error of name and place is open to much debate.) So there was no escape for the lively youngster; the wedding may have taken place at Luddington, two miles downstream from Stratford, but there are no documents to establish the facts. The church records were lost many centuries ago.

The newlyweds joined John and Mary Shakespeare in Henley Street. Within three years, three children were born; William Shakespeare, with visions of tales of imagination,

Shakespeare's Birthplace, Stratford-upon-Avon

154

Weeds

Crown'd with rank fumitor and furrow-weeds,
With burdocks, hemlock, nettles, cuckoo-flowers,
Darnel and all the idle weeds that grow
In our sustaining corn.

King Lear

There with fantastic garlands did she come,
Of crowflowers, nettles, daisies.

Hamlet

. . . I will go root away
The noisome weeds, which without profit suck
The soils fertility from wholesome flowers . . .

. . . our sea-walled garden, the whole land,
Is full of weeds, her fairest flowers chok'd up.

King Richard II

WILLIAM SHAKESPEARE

Anne Hathaway's Cottage, Shottery

seemed destined to spend his days as a small trader in a small Warwickshire town.

Five companies of actors came to Stratford in 1587, including that of the notable professional, Edward Alleyn; Shakespeare was bitten by the theatrical bug. He left the peaceful Warwickshire countryside of the Forest of Arden, left a wife and three children, and left a depressed and disgraced father who had just been expelled from the council for non-attendance. He packed his bags in Henley Street and crossed over Clopton Bridge, heading towards London for fame and fortune.

When he returned to Stratford as a wealthy man, he could have property of his own for the first time. He purchased the splendid New Place in 1597 and lived there until his death in 1616.

Today, Stratford is still a thriving market town but the Shakespeare industry is paramount. The landscape around, unenclosed in the sixteenth century, is of arable and pastoral farming in the vale of the Avon with coppices here and there of the old oaks of the Arden Forest. To the south, the horizon is of the Cotswold ridge and the hamlets of honey-coloured stone cottages cupped in the hollows.

The villages of the Shakespeares are to the north of Stratford where we will walk a few pathways after a short tour of the town.

The Seasons

It was a lover and his lass,
With a hey, and a ho, and a hey nonino,
That o'er the green cornfield did pass,
In the spring time, the only pretty ring time,
When birds do sing, hey ding a ding, ding;
Sweet lovers love the spring.

As You Like It

Where the bee sucks, there suck I:
In a cowslip's bell I lie;
There I couch when owls do cry.
On the bat's back I do fly
After summer merrily:
Merrily, merrily shall I live now
Under the blossom that hangs on the bough.

The Tempest

. . . an autumn was
That grew the more reaping; his delights
Were dolphin-like, they show'd his back above
The element they liv'd in. . .

Antony and Cleopatra

Therefore my age is as a lusty winter,
Frosty, but kindly.

As You Like It

WILLIAM SHAKESPEARE

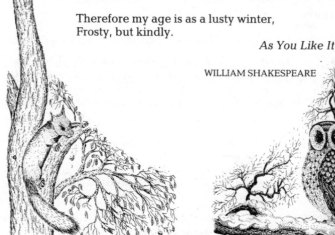

William Shakespeare Walk

1 Visit the church, the Grammar School, Shakespeare's Birthplace and other historic buildings in Stratford.

2 From Shakespeare's Birthplace in Henley Street, proceed to the A439, towards Evesham. Just before an old railway crossing turn right down a footpath at Evesham Place.

3 Cross an obsolete railway and recreation ground and continue to Shottery. Visit Anne Hathaway's Cottage.

4 Go along some estate roads towards the A422. Just before reaching the main road turn left down a footpath.

5 Keep on the same heading over a field through a gate. Keep ahead to the corner of a jutting field.

6 Climb the wire and walk with the hedge on the left. At the corner turn right to a gate. Go by the farm to a lane. Turn right to the A422.

7 Keep left for ½ mile. Before reaching the railings turn right through the gap. Climb the stile. Walk by a stream, soon crossing it to go along the other bank.

8 At the lane turn right for ½ mile. At the junction turn left through a gate. Follow the hedge to a wood; keep in the field.

9 Turn right then right again. Keep at the edge of the field around the corners until you come to a rough stile leading to the horse gallops.

10 Walk by the gallops to Wilmcote and Mary Arden's house.

11 Just past the church turn left down a vehicle drive and follow the farm road to the canal, then right on the tow path.

12 Before the lock-keeper's cottage, cross the canal. Climb the stile into the field.

13 Walk down the field to the gate. Aim to the right of the farm. Go along the drive to a lane.

14 Turn left to the canal and take the towpath to Stratford.

Information

The Shakespeare houses in Stratford are open all year round.

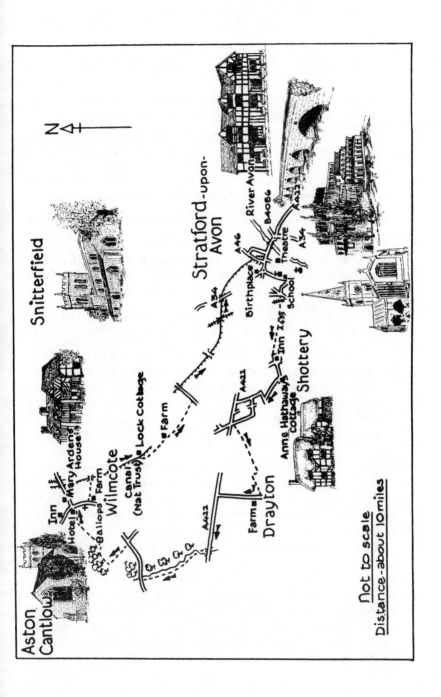

Aston Cantlow

Snitterfield

Inn

Hotel

Mary Ardens House

Gallops Farm

Wilmcote

Canal (Nat Trust)

Lock Cottage

Farm

A422

Drayton

Farm

A422

A34

Stratford-upon-Avon

River Avon

B4086

A46

Birthplace

Theatre

A422

A34

School

Inn A439

Anne Hathaway's cottage

Shottery

N

Not to scale
Distance - about 10 miles

On 20 April 1936, Dylan Thomas wrote to Vernon Watkins:

> I'm not a country man; I stand for, if anything, the aspidistra,
> the provincial drive, the morning café, the evening pub; I
> like to believe in the wide open space as the wrapping
> around walls, the windy boredom between house and house,
> hotel and cinema, bookshop and tube station.

This was the talk of a man from a city who, only a little over a
decade later, had settled in a delightful rural seaside retreat in
South Wales.

Dylan Thomas was born in Swansea on 27 October 1914. No
one could pretend the area around the semi-detached house at
5 Cwmdonkin Drive was pretty, although there were splendid
views across the bay, over the slate roofs and harbour to the
Mumbles rocks and lighthouse.

He declared that Swansea was

> an ugly town (or so it was and is to me) crawling, sprawling
> by a long and splendid curving shore where truant boys and
> sandfield boys and old men from nowhere beachcombed,
> idled and paddled, watched the dock-bound ships or the
> ships steaming away into wonder and India, magic and
> China, countries bright with oranges and loud with lions.

Dylan's father was an intellectual — a graduate who was to become Senior English Master at Swansea Grammar School. His
mother, Florrie, was from country stock; she was born in
Swansea but spent holidays and weekends with grandparents
in the countryside of Carmarthen.

Dylan attended Mrs Hole's School at Miradour Crescent. He
went, aged ten, to Swansea Grammar School. Although, to
everyone's surprise, he won a mile race at the school sports day,
he was to be troubled by lung illness from an early age.

The resultant time spent indoors was reckoned to be a factor
in his later literary success and his inherent love of words. He
became editor of the Swansea Grammar School magazine and
set his heart on becoming a professional writer.

The Town Hall, Laugharne

He left school in July 1931 and only took an examination in English. It was the time of the Depression but he found employment with the *South Wales Daily Post*. A short period as a proofreader was followed by an appointment as apprentice reporter.

Before he left school, Dylan had tried to start a periodical called *Prose and Verse*. The unsuccessful launch did not deter him and he tried to resurrect the publication a couple of years later; this time it would only feature the work of Welsh people.

Again the idea was stillborn — by this time Dylan's career as a newspaper reporter was over. It was said he would not learn the tool of trade of the pressman — shorthand. However, no doubt his long frequentation of the pubs of Swansea and his vivid imagination clouded any factual and accurate reporting.

This was a time of great literary output. In four years from 1930 to 1934 he composed over two hundred poems; many of these were considered to be some of his best. A number of poems were written at Rhossilli on the western tip of the Gower

161

Peninsula — a wild, rocky place where he would spend whole days followed by an eighteen-mile walk home. He submitted poetry to national weeklies and Sunday papers; his entries received almost instant recognition and praise.

The young poet's only other income at this time was a few pounds earned acting with the Mumbles Stage Society and writing plays for the Little Theatre.

Dylan started corresponding with the authoress Pamela Hansford Johnson in September 1933 — she had written to him to express admiration for a poem. A frequent exchange of letters was followed by many meetings in London and South Wales and a hint of romance. In 1934, he moved to London and earned a meagre income reviewing books. Although Pamela Hansford Johnson and Dylan remained good friends, they decided that their paths were diverting with Dylan inevitably treading a fast Bohemian way to raffish parties and pubs.

He was to meet his future wife Caitlin Macnamara at a pub party in 1936; Caitlin was an assertive youngster. At seventeen she had run away with her friend to London to seek a stage career. After dancing lessons, she became a chorus girl at the Palladium. Dylan and Caitlin were invited to Laugharne to stay with the novelist, Richard Hughes, at his house that nestled against the ruined castle. Dylan had said it was love at first sight — they talked of marriage even at the first meeting. The registry office wedding followed some weeks spent in Cornwall in the summer of 1937.

They lived with Caitlin's mother in a pretty place, New Inn House at Ringwood, and seemed to favour the country life; happy excursions were made on bicycles into the New Forest. Next year the couple left for Wales, at first to live with Dylan's parents, then to their village of early romance, Laugharne. Their house was called Sea View, a 'tall and dignified house at the "posh" end of town'.

'Posh end of town' it may have been, but money for the Thomas family was very short. Dylan continued to write his poems and his work was widely reviewed. He earned a modest income, in addition, by reviewing thrillers for the *London Morning Post* and general fiction for the *New English Weekly*.

The Thomases' first child Llewelyn, was born in Hampshire in 1939. The country provided the right atmosphere for the writing of two works, the book of poems *The World I Breathe* and *Portrait of the Artist as a Young Dog*.

Excused National Service early in the Second World War due to acute asthma, Dylan's excess drinking and debts increased. There was some relief with work on documentary films.

Another child arrived; by 1945 the family was living at New Quay, Cardiganshire, which Dylan drew as background for his famous radio talk 'Quite Early One Morning'.

He took to the seaside life; 'Poem in October', completed towards the end of the war, has some splendid descriptive lines of country reminiscences; an earlier poem of this title appeared in the BBC magazine *The Listener*. From 1937 he had often contributed to BBC programmes. There were some now often-read pieces like the charming 'A Child's Christmas in Wales' and 'Return Journey'. Poetry reading on the Third Programme provided a further regular income.

But all this time Dylan was at heart a Bohemian. There was a period spent in the summer of 1947 in Italy with his family. It was not a happy time; Dylan, knowing no Italian, missed the verbose conversation of his own land. On his return, there was the start of ever more lengthy times of despair with drink being a regular remedy.

The family's friendship with Margaret Taylor (wife of historian Professor A. J. P. Taylor) resulted in the generous provision of accommodation for the Thomases at South Leigh,

The Boat House, Laugharne

Oxfordshire. Dylan was offered work again on film scripts in addition to radio broadcasts; although earning well at this time, he spent well and even begged for advances. 'The bills are wailing', he once wrote. Life at South Leigh was tough with no electricity and only cold water.

In March 1949, Margaret Taylor purchased The Boat House at Laugharne and offered it to Dylan and Caitlin. It was a spectacular setting overlooking the estuary of the River Taf and Laugharne evoked many happy memories of earlier days. Two months after the move to The Boat House, a third child was born. The times might have been well if the family's finances could have been managed. In 1950, Dylan was invited to America by the American poet, John Malcolm Brinnin.

Dylan was to make two appearances at the Poetry Centre and subsequent poetry reading engagements. (The success of the trip by the flamboyant and ebullient man from Wales was followed by three further visits.) However, by the end of the trip he failed to keep any of the sizeable fees to provide relief from his debts at home and he could not easily reawaken the enthusiasm to compose new verse.

He was not unproductive and in the afternoons worked in the little green toolhouse perched on a clifftop above The Boat House. He could look over the bay and St John's Hill, the rippling sea and the ribbed sand to seek the inspiration for 'Poem on his Birthday'.

There were further trips to the United States in 1952 and 1953. On the 1953 visit, the world première of the play 'Under Milk Wood' was performed at Boston. This work is considered the masterpiece of Dylan Thomas; it is an amalgam of life in the mythical Welsh village of Llareggub (perhaps Laugharne).

On his return to The Boat House, Dylan gave thought to the request for the submission of a libretto for a Stravinsky opera score. With increasing fainting turns he was advised by his doctor that total abstinence from alcohol was necessary to survive. The attraction of high fees for poetry readings attracted the unfit Dylan to America for a fourth time late in 1953. There were further heavy drinking sessions in spite of illness and nausea; when he collapsed, he was rushed to a New York hospital. Caitlin arrived by air but the poet was in a coma. He died on 9 November. His body was returned to Laugharne, the 'timeless beautiful' town, and he was buried in a simple grave in the hillside graveyard of St Martin's Church.

Poem in October

It was my thirtieth year to heaven
Woke to my hearing from harbour and neighbour wood
   And the mussel pooled and the heron
        Priested shore
        The morning beckon
With water praying and call of seagull and rook
And the knock of sailing boats on the net webbed wall
        Myself to set foot
           That second
   In the sleeping town and set forth.

   My birthday began with the water-
Birds and the birds of the winged trees flying my name
   Above the farms and the white horses
        And I rose
        In rainy autumn
And walked abroad in a shower of all my days.
High tide and the heron dived when I took the road
        Over the border
           And the gates
   Of the town closed as the town awoke.

   A springful of larks in a rolling
Cloud and the roadside bushes brimming with whistling
   Blackbirds and the sun of October
        Summery
        On the hill's shoulder,
Here were fond climates and sweet singers suddenly
Come in the morning where I wandered and listened
        To the rain wringing
           Wind blow cold
   In the wood faraway under me.

DYLAN THOMAS

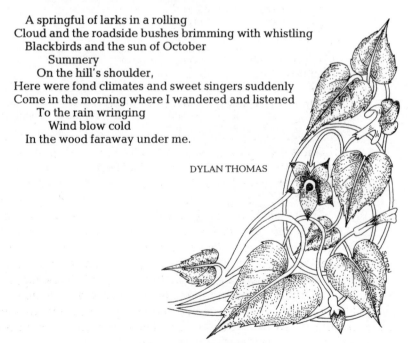

165

Fern Hill

Now as I was young and easy under the apple boughs
About the lilting house and happy as the grass was green,
   The night above the dingle starry,
    Time let me hail and climb
  Golden in the heydays of his eyes,
And honoured among wagons I was prince of the apple towns
And once below a time I lordly had the trees and leaves
    Trail with daisies and barley
  Down the rivers of the windfall light.

And as I was green and carefree, famous among the barns
About the happy yard and singing as the farm was home,
   In the sun that is young once only,
    Time let me play and be
  Golden in the mercy of his means,
And green and golden I was huntsman and herdsman, the calves
Sang to my horn, the foxes on the hills barked clear and cold,
    And the sabbath rang slowly
  In the pebbles of the holy streams.

All the sun long it was running, it was lovely, the hay
Fields high as the house, the tunes from the chimneys, it was air
   And playing, lovely and watery
    And fire green as grass.
  And nightly under the simple stars
As I rode to sleep the owls were bearing the farm away,
All the moon long I heard, blessed among stables, the night-jars
   Flying with the ricks, and the horses
    Flashing into the dark.

And then to awake, and the farm, like a wanderer white
With the dew, come back, the cock on his shoulder: it was all
    Shining, it was Adam and maiden,
       The sky gathered again
    And the sun grew round that very day.
So it must have been after the birth of the simple light
In the first, spinning place, the spellbound horses walking warm
    Out of the whinnying green stable
      On to the fields of praise.

And honoured among foxes and pheasants by the gay house
Under the new made clouds and happy as the heart was long
    In the sun born over and over,
      I ran my heedless ways,
    My wishes raced through the house high hay
And nothing I cared, at my sky blue trades, that time allows
In all his tuneful turning so few and such morning songs
    Before the children green and golden
      Follow him out of grace.

Nothing I cared, in the lamb white days, that time would take me
Up to the swallow thronged loft by the shadow of my hand,
    In the moon that is always rising,
      Nor that riding to sleep
    I should hear him fly with the high fields
And wake to the farm forever fled from the childless land.
Oh as I was young and easy in the mercy of his means,
      Time held me green and dying
    Though I sang in my chains like the sea.

DYLAN THOMAS

Dylan Thomas Walk

1. From Laugharne Town Hall *(built 1746)* walk downhill. Pass the castle *(where Dylan and Caitlin stayed)*.

2. Swing left by the car park. Go over the bridge (River Corran) and walk below the cliffs. Just before The Boat House climb the steps to Dylan's Walk.

3. Turn right to Dylan's work hut and The Boat House Museum. Keep on the track through vehicle barriers and woods. Stay in the same direction through rough pastures.

4. At the border of the River Taf the path bears left to a stile almost hidden behind a tree.

5. Aim for the farm buildings and go through the gates. Keep to the left of the farmhouse to the drive.

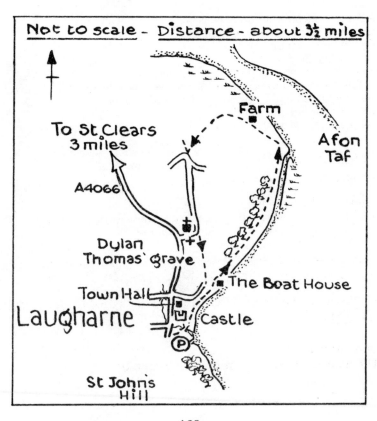

The Bay, Laugharne

6 Walk along the drive and through the gates to a lane. Turn left.

7 Proceed downhill to St Martin's Church (*fourteenth century*). Pass through a metal kissing gate on the right to the churchyard.

8 By the church building veer left to cross a footbridge to the new churchyard.

9 Visit Dylan Thomas' grave which is marked by a simple white cross.

10 Continue to the kissing gate at the top end of the graveyard to a vehicle track. Turn right.

11 The track becomes a footpath and leads to the road. Turn right to Victoria Street and Laugharne.

Information
The Boat House is open from April to October.

Shropshire has one or two scars to sadden the eye. Quarrying seems to be allowed in the most exquisite countryside and Telford, like all new towns, will take many more years of weathering to soften the coldness and harshness of its appearance. However, much of the country remains completely unspoilt and just as Mary Webb knew it before the impact of motoring for all. Her love of Shropshire is mirrored in her books, which are placed (with names disguised) in this corner of England. The giant's teeth, set on a hilltop that we call the Stiperstones, were called the Diafol Mountains, the towns of Church Stretton and Bishop's Castle were Shepwardine and Mallard's Keep, and so on.

Mary Webb knew, as though by instinct, the legends and customs of Shropshire; she lived among the hardy folk of the Welsh borderlands. All the aspects of the way of life with which she was familiar were brought into her novels.

Mary Gladys Webb was born in 1881 in the village of Leighton. It was a family custom to use her second Christian name so she was known as Gladys until after her marriage. Some miles from Shrewsbury the village nestles below the slopes of that mysterious conical shaped hill, The Wrekin; nearby is the sinuous River Severn. To Mary the high hill was one of those 'inviolable places', those 'changeless heights'.

Her house was called Leighton Lodge — red brick and ivy covered with tall chimneys. Her father, George Meredith, ran a small boarding school from the house. Here, boys were prepared for entrance to public schools or military establishments.

George Meredith was said to have been cultured and witty. He also wrote poetry and was remembered for his kind disposition — virtues which were passed on to Mary. He loved the countryside intensely. He had married Sarah Alice Scott — like him from a strong Church of England and moderately wealthy family — in 1880. The following year Mary was born; she was a spring child, a child of nature.

When she was fifteen months old the family moved a few miles westward to Much Wenlock, an ancient borough which, said Mary Webb, 'had not since the day it fell asleep, changed its coat, its hosen or its hat'. The Merediths, now quite pros-

Much Wenlock

perous, purchased The Grange, a fine country estate that included the house, a lodge and a farm. Its situation was splendid for the nature-loving family, in a green vale on the dipping slopes of Wenlock Edge.

Another five children were born during the fifteen years the Merediths were at The Grange. The father and elder child loved the isolated life close to nature with all its moods. Mother Alice was not so at one with her surroundings.

The poetry of George Meredith, serious and with a close concern always with the correctness of the form of the verse, no doubt influenced Mary's work. But George could never express with that intense personal feeling, the intimate feeling for nature that was identified with his daughter's descriptions and lines.

From her window at The Grange Mary looked out across meadows and woodlands to wide vistas of the Edge. Nature came to her very door and there were always the farm animals — the cows and horses (especially a grey pony) and poultry which her father kept. There was a gardener, a coachman and cowman — characters that would all prove models for folk in

171

The Grange, Wenlock Edge

her later novels. The cowman was John Lloyd, who was called 'Owd Blossom'.

Later she recalled her early days at The Grange when she went

into the cornfields that lay beneath the vasty blue peace of the sky like creatures satisfied and at rest. There would be small birds about, making low contented cries and soft songs. There would be a rustling breeze and rooks far up the sky, and a second bloom of pale gold flowers on the honeysuckle against the blue.

George Meredith expanded his boarding school at The Grange and also enjoyed the life of a gentleman farmer. He sketched with some skill — Mary inherited this talent also and liked especially to paint plants and flowers.

Mary's formal education was started by her father. She was also taught by a governess, Mrs Lyons, who was a friend of Alice Meredith. There would be long walks with her father in the fields and woods near The Grange and further distances to the bleak heights of the Long Mynd and the Stiperstones. They would also drive in the brougham along the ridgetop of Wenlock Edge to the glorious countryside unfolding at their feet. On these trips Mary would hear of the countless local legends and superstitions. There were tales about Wild Edric whose ghost is said to haunt the hills. He was a fighter at the time of the Norman Conquest. On top of the Stiperstones is the foreboding rock of the Devil's Chair which appears and disappears in the mist. Not far from The Grange is Major's Leap, a cliff on the Wenlock Edge over which Major Smallman plunged on his horse during the Civil War; the animal perished but the Cavalier soldier was caught by a crab-apple tree and thus escaped from his Roundhead pursuers. He had set out from the gabled grey stone Wilderhope Manor, a lonely house above Corvedale, and haunted, with secret rooms and escape routes. These artifacts no doubt delight the young people who now visit the building (Wilderhope is a youth hostel, owned by the National Trust.)

Mary's wanderings also taught her about the folklore of the borderlands. She was aware of 'a permanence, continuity in country life which makes the lapse of centuries seem of little moment', (as recorded in the foreword of one of her books). There is no doubt that her early years at Much Wenlock gave her the formulative experiences on which she was to develop her creative work.

Mary always remembered the influence and encouragement of her father. George Meredith called her from an early age his 'Precious Bane'. This was to be the title of one of her finest books. However, Mary did not just slavishly follow her father in all respects, but showed her independence in several ways. She became a vegetarian, and although her parents were enthusiastic members of the county hunt she abhored all blood sports. It was on a hunt that misfortune struck — Alice Meredith was thrown from her horse and suffered a serious spinal injury. She remained an invalid for the rest of her life. To the Meredith children she became a remote and formidable mother.

When Mary was fourteen, it was decided her education should be continued at a boarding school — 'finishing schools' to impress on young ladies the correct social graces were popular in late Victorian times. So Mary Webb was sent away from her beloved Shropshire and its countryside to Mrs Walmsley's Finishing School at Southport.

While his daughter was away, George Meredith became ill and closed his school. It was decided to sell the farm, then The Grange itself. With Alice's incapacity the thriftiness of the household deteriorated and, with the loss of the school and farm income, a move was made to a less costly home.

Wenlock Priory

The house at Stanton-upon-Hine Heath was north of Shrewsbury, some fifteen miles from Much Wenlock. It was then called The Woodlands: today, it is Hencourt Manor. It is a remote place 'five miles from anything' and was to be the home for Mary Webb for nine years.

These were difficult years; with Alice confined to the upstairs rooms, Mary managed the house and assisted in the tuition of her brothers and sisters. Her relaxation was trips to the countryside — comparatively flat around Stanton and suited to the bicycle that she bought — and the pony and trap. Mary would often disappear for a week or so, taking her paper and writing pens and pencils. Only her father would know of her whereabouts.

She was at that time closely associated with the local St Andrew's Church and sang in the choir with her father and taught at the Sunday school. She distributed the parish magazine and it was in this that she saw her first published poems. (We still have 'Spring' to appreciate her growing skill with words.)

With the stern Alice confined away from the living rooms, the house was a happy home. However, Alice made something of a sudden recovery. Her re-emergence created a dreary atmosphere and Mary became ever more serious and quiet and seeking solitude. She became pallid and anaemic; at the same time there were long cycle rides and walks into her beloved rural ways. The mental and physical exhaustion showed itself in the onset of Graves Disease. The first six months were desperate times; when she was stronger she was brought downstairs so she could gaze over the lands she knew so well. As her health gradually improved she began to write essays which were, after her fame, published as *The Spring of Joy*. In view of her poor appearance due to the illness, the optimism and appreciation of lovely things contained in the essays are remarkable.

There was, in 1901, another move for the Merediths. This time George bought the ivy-clad Mill House at Maesbrook, only a mile or so from Shrewsbury. (The house has now been demolished.) In time the walks were resumed, an especial favourite route being to the top of Lyth Hill, lonely, windswept with bracken and wood slopes.

Mary began to play bridge with enthusiasm and regularly visited Shrewsbury library and lectures at local schools. She was an avid reader and, with the added mental energy of writing again, was never in good health.

Early in 1909, George Meredith died after a fall. More than other members of the family, Mary, because of their close affinity with the countryside and folklore, was desolate. Her only real consolation was in the solitude of her poetry and later the lone creativity of her prose fiction.

She had some minor literary success and *A Cedar Rose*, a short story, appeared in *Country Life*. But disappointment was to follow. With high hopes she had sent off her collected essays to publishers. The rejection was tempered by her growing friendship with Henry Webb, a schoolmaster in Shrewsbury. Love blossomed and despite further illness, Mary Meredith became Mary Webb in June 1912.

The first two years of married life were spent in Weston-super-Mare. She began to put the thoughts in her imagination of her home county on paper and the seeds of *The Golden Arrow* were sown. The setting of the novel was to be Wilderhope and the Stiperstones.

In 1914 Henry resigned his teaching post and the couple returned to Shropshire. They took the tenancy of Rose Cottage, a detached house at Pontesbury, below the slopes of the Long Mynd. The deliberate intention was to return to nature — he to translate poetry from other languages, she to continue with *The Golden Arrow*. For her novel Mary started to draw on characters in her memory: John Arden was modelled on her father, and she wove into the work about thirty local legends and superstitions.

The Webbs discouraged callers and grew their own produce. Mary worked hard in the large garden and, although she gave to poor local folk, she began to find she had surplus produce. At first she sold to the stall holders; later, with a touch of her mother's thrift, she took a stall herself, often walking the nine miles there and nine back. Mary could observe and submerge herself among the country-folk and, after the publication of *The Golden Arrow*, she became a local curiosity.

The 'simple life' proved simpler to dream about than to practise and money became increasingly short. Henry did some occasional tutoring and also worked as a rate collector. Reluctantly they moved in 1916 to a smaller and cheaper house, The Mills, on the Stiperstones ridge. The financial situation did not improve and Henry took a post as master at The King's School, Chester. The Webbs lived with Alice Meredith during the week and returned to the peace of The Mills at weekends.

Work on *Gone to Earth* continued. This was a romantic tale about hunting, in which Mary Webb's hatred of bloodsports is evident (as is her knowledge of legends and country-lore).

Henry obtained a new post at the Priory School, Shrewsbury, which again necessitated a move. However, this time it was to her well-remembered Lyth Hill. They rented at first, then planned and built their own Spring Cottage.

The next book, *The House in Dormer Forest*, received disappointing reviews and was often called 'gloomy'. Mary's depression and illness with a recurrence of Graves Disease worsened. It was suggested a change of environment would help and that her literary career would be improved by living in London. Henry applied for and obtained a job at King Alfred School, Golders Green.

The beloved cottage on Lyth Hill was retained for weekend visits. The London cure did not work and Mary's longing for Shropshire increased. She worked on *Seven for a Secret*, but

The Elf

Early there come travelling
  On market day
Old men and young men
  From far away
With red fruits of the orchard
  And dark fruits of the hill,
Dew-fresh garden stuff
  And mushrooms chill,
Honey from the brown skep,
  Brown eggs, and posies
Of gillyflowers and Lent lilies
  And blush roses . . .

MARY WEBB

177

the creative flow was not there and it was decided that she would stay alone at Spring Cottage; but she missed her husband and the strain told. The novel was completed (dedicated, with his permission, to Thomas Hardy). The strain on the relationship between Mary and Henry developed, accentuated by financial difficulties. Again Mary returned to London, with the couple always spending holidays in Shropshire.

It was during the summer visit in 1923 that Mary gathered detail and inspiration for her greatest work, *Precious Bane*. The writing took three months and the reviews were good, one calling her 'a genius'.

Success with the critics did not bring happiness; her marriage to Henry was disintegrating and he preferred the London life. The difficulties were exacerbated by bad health and emotional and mental distress but she continued her creative work with the novel *Armour wherein he Trusted,* and rather sad poems.

There were distraught pleas for money to her publishers and another woman, Kathleen, was in Henry's life. There was self-neglect and loneliness but a bright spot in 1927 was a personal letter of praise for *Precious Bane* from the Prime Minister, Stanley Baldwin.

Mary returned to London, hoping forlornly to heal her broken marriage. She had a fall and it was agreed that she would go to a nursing home at St Leonards-on-Sea. Here she died on 8 October 1927.

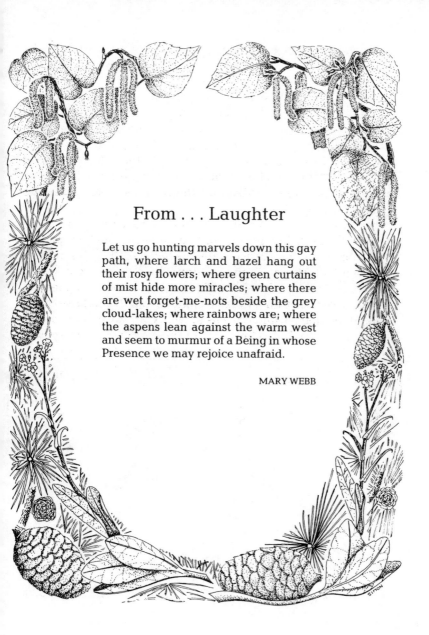

From . . . Laughter

Let us go hunting marvels down this gay path, where larch and hazel hang out their rosy flowers; where green curtains of mist hide more miracles; where there are wet forget-me-nots beside the grey cloud-lakes; where rainbows are; where the aspens lean against the warm west and seem to murmur of a Being in whose Presence we may rejoice unafraid.

MARY WEBB

179

Mary Webb Walk

1 From Much Wenlock (*Priory, sixteenth-century Guildhall, old inns*) walk south along the A458.

2 Take the first lane on the right (Callaughton). After ¾ mile turn right along a farm drive.

3 Keep on the track to swing right past a farm.

4 Climb up a rise to the B4378. *In the valley below is Mary Webb's home, The Grange.*

5 Turn left on the B4378. After ½ mile take the lane on the right. The path starts on the left after 300 yards. (If it is blocked keep on the B4378 to pick up the proper path through a gate on the right.)

6 The path becomes a hedged track to join the B4378. Turn right to Bourton.

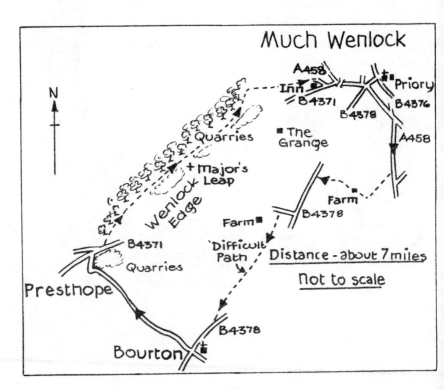

7 At the crossroads turn right to climb Wenlock Edge and the B4371. *In Corvedale, a few miles to the left, is Wilderhope Manor.*

8 Turn right on the B4371. Just past the junction a bridleway (rather hidden) starts on the left.

9 Keep along the clear track for 2 miles through the woods to a green 'road'.

10 The 'road' goes by some old quarries to the B4371. Turn left to the A458 and Much Wenlock.

WILLIAM WORDSWORTH

Wordsworth was a great traveller; he liked to tour Britain and further afield, journeying to the continent and courting a French girl. But always he returned to the countryside of his childhood, the English Lake District.

The craggy bracken-coated hills, the idyllic stretches of water in valleys scooped out during the Ice Age, the misted peaks of mountains like Helvellyn and Great Gable — this is the landscape over which the poet loved to roam, sometimes with his sister, sometimes alone.

Throughout Wordsworth's life, even in his later years when he could go anywhere by carriage, he preferred to walk. He often undertook long distances and would think nothing of twelve-mile hikes over the mountains.

The Classical Age was drawing to a close; Wordsworth was one of the early English Romantics who provided the escapism during times which were often troubled and revolutionary. These writers were to show the finer qualities of mankind. The subject of much of Wordsworth's verse turned away from artificial formality and urban ways to the wild splendours of nature; the style too was radical — simple and readily acceptable to the ordinary man.

The countryside was continuously his inspiration, not only the Cumbrian lands but also other parts of Britain like the western counties — Dorset, Somerset and Gloucestershire — and Yorkshire and Scotland. Even before Wordsworth's death in 1850, admirers were journeying to Lakeland to see at first hand the peaceful places which moved him to such heights of creativity. They came like pilgrims travelling to their shrines — and still they come today.

Wordsworth's parents were married in 1766. John Wordsworth was a solicitor and was agent to a Cumberland landowner, Sir Thomas Lowther. His young bride, Anne Cookson, daughter of a tradesman, was eighteen. They were provided with a rather splendid house at Cockermouth. Five children were born here; the second was William on 7 April 1770 and his sister Dorothy, who was to influence his life so much, arrived on Christmas Day the following year.

Their house was bordered by the River Derwent and from an

Ullswater

early age William and Dorothy explored the meanderings of the river and the natural world of the bankside. These times were to be recalled in the autobiographical poem *The Prelude.* The children also visited the port of Whitehaven where Uncle Richard Wordsworth was the Collector of Customs.

William attended the village school at Penrith where another student was Mary Hutchinson who was to be William's wife. When William was seven his mother died; his father could not cope alone and although he encouraged them to read and learn from books, William and his brothers were sent to the Cookson grandparents at Penrith. For nine years William was not to see his sister Dorothy, who was brought up at Halifax.

In 1779 William started as a boarder at Hawkshead Grammar School. (He actually stayed most of the time nearby in the cottage of the kindly Ann Tyson.) It was a fortuitous choice of school, for the headmaster was William Taylor who loved poetry. At the happy establishment he urged William to appreciate and write poems. There were also the sports of the countryside to enjoy and William especially was attracted by the pleasures of walking at night.

His father died in 1783 (when William was thirteen). Apart

from the holidays at the grandparents the next four years were spent with Ann Tyson. She was to be mother in everything but name, encouraging him in his studies.

In 1787, after beginning a romantic poem, 'The Vale of Esthwaite', Wordsworth started at St John's College, Cambridge. He missed the mountains and hills of Lakeland but worked steadily and continued with the writing of verse. He realised his vocation was poetry when he met a poor, down-and-out soldier on one of his nocturnal rambles. His verses were not to be in the classical mould but of nature, humanity and the ordinary folk. He wrote 'An Evening Walk' for his sister.

After the fall of the Bastille in 1789, Wordsworth decided to go with a college friend, Robert Jones, on a three-month walking holiday through France to Switzerland and Italy. They covered enormous distances and in the intervening stops had long discussions with Frenchmen celebrating the Revolution; Wordsworth was very sympathetic to their cherished ideals.

After returning to Cambridge he completed his final examinations and then had to think about a career. His uncle, William Cookson, a Fellow at St John's, considered he should enter the Church; Wordsworth would have preferred a legal or military career.

To try to come to a decision, Wordsworth went to London then walked in North Wales with Robert Jones. He was being pressed by the Cookson grandparents to choose an occupation. In August 1791, however, a large debt owed by Lord Lonsdale to Wordsworth's late father was ordered (after a court action) to be repaid to the Wordsworth children. Although the money was not in fact paid at this time the affair allowed Wordsworth a breathing space to settle on a career. He went to France again, ostensibly to learn the language thoroughly.

He lodged at a house in Orleans and there met Annette Vallon. There was a passionate involvement by the youthful Wordsworth and Annette became pregnant by him. He fully intended to bring her to England at some future date and to submit himself for ordination by the Church. Before he left France in late 1792, he was convinced he was now a revolutionary, a patriot. In December 1792, after he had departed, his daughter Caroline was born.

To obtain some money, Wordsworth found a publisher for An Evening Walk' and *Descriptive Sketches,* which was a word picture of his earlier tour in France. To his consternation, however, war broke out between France and England.

A friendship developed between Wordsworth and the wealthy Calvert brothers, William and Raisley. (William Calvert had been at school with Wordsworth.) The Calverts loaned Wordsworth a farmhouse near Keswick for some weeks in 1794; for the first time William and Dorothy set up home together and they resumed their walking excursions.

The next year Raisley died and left Wordsworth £900. Wordsworth journeyed to London and stayed with Basil Montagu, a young lawyer whom he had met at Cambridge. Wordsworth was depressed and frustrated with the war against France dragging on, which thwarted his plans to bring Annette and his daughter Caroline to England.

Through Montagu, Wordsworth met John Pinney. Pinney's father was a wealthy Bristol merchant and owned a splendid ivy-clad house called Racedown near Lyme Regis. The house was rarely used and Pinney offered it without payment for the use of Wordsworth and his sister.

Mary Hutchinson renewed her friendship with Wordsworth

Tintern Abbey

— they had not met since his romance with Annette in France. At the same time Wordsworth became acquainted with Robert Southey and Samuel Taylor Coleridge (who married sisters Edith and Sara Fricker). Coleridge was to play an important part in Wordsworth's later life. He admired Wordsworth's poems and was sent new work such as 'Salisbury Plain' and 'The Borderers' to read.

Wordsworth and his sister came to live in some delightful countryside near Coleridge. Their mansion, Alfoxden, was taken for a year and was at the foot of the Quantock Hills in Somerset, an ideal place for the poet to overcome his depression and to recapture his inspirational spirit. A particularly productive tour was to the beautiful Wye Valley where 'Lines Written a Few Miles above Tintern Abbey' was composed.

Coleridge (with his 'The Ancient Mariner') and Wordsworth's latest poems were combined in a work *Lyrical Ballads* to obtain funds for a proposed visit to Germany to further their knowledge of the language and thereby the literature of the country.

However, with the inclement weather, the tourists met few people and the trip was not a success although during this time Wordsworth did begin the long poem *The Prelude*. On his return to England he stayed with the Hutchinson brothers and sisters on a farm at Sockburn-on-Tees. Again he met Mary and he must now have considered her as a future wife with Annette being unattainable in alien France.

Wordsworth and Coleridge resumed their walking expeditions. One of their trips was to Grasmere and it was there that Wordsworth came across Dove Cottage, which he later described enthusiastically to his sister Dorothy.

Wordsworth and Dorothy walked most of the way to the cottage. They climbed over the hills in the savage winter weather of December 1799 to the little house that was once an inn (The Dove and Olive Branch) — a charming spot overlooking the lake.

Mary was a frequent visitor and one of Wordsworth's poems written at this time was dedicated to 'my sweet Mary'. However, in December 1801 letters from Annette and his daughter were smuggled across the Channel from Napoleon's France.

A new edition of *Lyrical Ballads* was prepared, again combined with work by Coleridge in the first volume. It was published in 1801. Coleridge's life was now beginning to de-

Morning After a Storm

There was a roaring in the wind all night;
The rain came heavily and fell in floods;
But now the sun is rising calm and bright;
The birds are singing in the distant woods;
Over his own sweet voice the stock-dove
broods;
The Jay makes answer as the Magpie chatters;
And all the air is filled with pleasant noise of
waters.

All things that love the sun are out of doors;
The sky rejoices in the morning's birth;
The grass is bright with rain-drops — on the
moors
The hare is running races in her mirth;
And with her feet she from the plashy earth
Raises a mist, that, glittering in the sun,
Runs with her all the way, wherever she doth
run.

WILLIAM WORDSWORTH

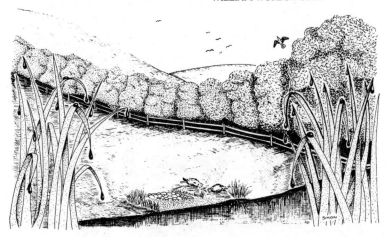

187

The Daffodils

I wandered lonely as a cloud
That floats on high o'er vales and hills,
When all at once I saw a crowd,
A host of golden daffodils,
Beside the lake, beneath the trees,
Fluttering and dancing in the breeze.

Continuous as the stars that shine
And twinkle on the milky way,
They stretched in never-ending line
Along the margin of a bay:
Ten thousand saw I at a glance
Tossing their heads in sprightly dance.

The waves beside them danced, but they
Out-did the sparkling waves in glee:
A poet could not but be gay
In such a jocund company!
I gazed — and gazed — but little thought
What wealth the show to me had brought.

For oft, when on my couch I lie
In vacant or in pensive mood,
They flash upon that inward eye
Which is the bliss of solitude;
And then my heart with pleasure fills,
And dances with the daffodils.

WILLIAM WORDSWORTH

teriorate; with severe depression he began to take opium and his marriage was failing when he fell in love with Mary Hutchinson's sister, Sara.

With the death of Lord Lonsdale the old debt was at last paid by his heir to the children of John Wordsworth. William and Dorothy each inherited £1,600; they were now comparatively wealthy and could afford to make preparations to journey to France to see Annette and Caroline.

They spent a month at Calais and Annette agreed not to press her claim for Wordsworth's hand in marriage. In a little over a month Wordsworth at last married his old sweetheart Mary Hutchinson. Strangely, Dorothy did not attend the ceremony and stranger still it was a threesome (including Dorothy) that left together in the carriage following the wedding reception.

Wordsworth now had two devoted ladies to satisfy his every whim. William and Mary's first child, John, was soon to be born— in June 1803. This did not deter Wordsworth from his travels. By August he was off to Scotland with Dorothy and Coleridge, visiting places associated with Burns and calling on Sir Walter Scott.

Wordsworth named his second child after his sister; she was destined to become yet another assiduous helper to the poet. Meanwhile, in the same year, 1804, his sister-in-law Sara arrived to swell the size of the household at Dove Cottage.

Wordsworth, composing mainly on his long jaunts over the hills, completed his autobiographical *The Prelude* and also wrote many sad lines after the death at sea of his brother John.

In 1807 *Poems in Two Volumes* was published. The simplicity and commonplace subject matter made Wordsworth the butt for literary critics of the day who were accustomed to the stilted classical style of verse.

By 1808, with the growing household comprising the Wordsworth family (there were now four children) and acquaintances, Dove Cottage was no longer large enough and a move was made to Allan Bank, Grasmere. However, with the shortage of funds, and Coleridge's departure following a tiff with Wordsworth, another move was made after three years — Grasmere Parsonage near the church was small and less expensive to run. Sadness was soon to come to the house for in a single year, two of the Wordsworth children died.

In 1813 the family finances improved when Wordsworth was given the post of Distributor of Stamps for Westmorland by

Lord Lonsdale. Although not a sinecure, the duties allowed plenty of time for walking and writing. With the increased security and wealth the Wordsworths left Grasmere village. Rydal Mount on a spectacular site overlooking Rydal Water was to be Wordsworth's home for the remainder of his life, although it is generally accepted that the inspirational spur and the simple verse style had now gone. Perhaps the ridicule of the critics was eating into the creative soul; perhaps it was sadness at the loss of Annette or the decline of the great friendship with Coleridge.

By the time Wordsworth was settled at Rydal Mount no longer was he the zealous reformer proclaiming liberty and change, but the staunch entrenched salaried upholder of the conservative establishment.

With daughter Dora now a constant companion, Wordsworth had four women in the house to look after his needs. But in 1829 Dorothy suffered a severe illness and ill-advisedly continued to walk the long distances she had easily managed in earlier days. The result was that Dorothy was an invalid for the rest of her life.

Mary's sister Sara died in 1835; Wordsworth's health was good apart from failing eyesight. He wrote long works, somewhat distant from the previous simple prose but still inspired by lengthy walks throughout Cumbria, and in 1838 his *Sonnets* (which included a total of 415) was published.

After the death of Southey in 1843, Wordsworth, although at first refusing, accepted the offer of the Poet Laureateship. However, the retreat from his old revolutionary visions is exemplified by his attempts to keep the new railways, which would convey hosts of working folk, away from the area of Lakeland. How ironic that in later years these railways brought so many visitors to the places associated with the poet.

Another of Wordsworth's former women helpers, his much-loved daughter Dora, died in 1847 after developing consumption. The poet in his remorse was comforted by his devoted Mary and was to live another three years.

William Wordsworth, one of England's greatest poets, passed away on St George's Day, 23 April 1850, and was buried in the churchyard at Grasmere.

William Wordsworth Walk

1 From the car park on the A591 midway between Grasmere and Rydal cross the road.

2 The path starts at White Moss picnic place. Go down the steps.

3 Veer right to the footbridge to cross the River Rothay. Keep ahead through the woods.

4 Through a gate in a wall turn left and drop down the hill to cross the brook. Walk at the edge of Rydal Water.

5 Keep on the path by the lake. Cross the river and climb to join the A591. Turn right past Dora's Field then left on the lane to the church.

6 Go to the top of the lane to Rydal Mount and the car park. Turn left along the path (Grasmere).

7 Keep ahead through the woods to join a vehicle track. By the pool turn left to the starting place.

8 Retrace your steps to the gate in the wall and turn right. Walk by Grasmere for ½ mile. Turn left to the stile and lane.

9 Turn right to Grasmere village and visit Wordsworth's grave. Proceed to the A591. Cross to the lane to Dove Cottage.

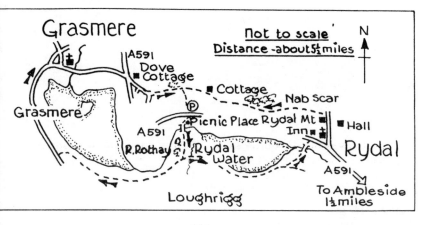

Rydal Mount

10 Keep ahead past the cottage. Go left at the junction along a vehicle way to the previous pool.

11 Retrace earlier steps to the car park on the A591.

Information
Dove Cottage and Rydal Mount are open from April to October.